HEALING VISIONS

True Stories of Healing through Divine Intervention
First-aid for the Soul

KATHERINE CONNON

Sólás

Sólás Press books may be ordered through booksellers or by contacting:

Sólás Press
Newport
Co. Mayo
Ireland.
joy@thescepticalhealer.com

ISBN: 978-0-9567999-0-6   Healing Visions - First-Aid for the Soul   Hardback x

ISBN: 978-0-9567999-1-3   Healing Visions - First-Aid for the Soul   Paperback x

Printed in Ireland

Mike Howard had a fatal heart attack on the 19th September 2010. I can just imagine his joy, when so many loving arms received him in Heaven.

CONTENTS

ACKNOWLEDGMENTS

I am grateful to the many people who have contributed to the gestation of this book. This publication's genesis dates back many years, and many people encouraged me throughout this process to write about the wonderful experiences they and my other clients have had. I cannot mention all those who contributed to this book, as there are just too many. I cried and laughed with so many wonderful people over the last twenty-plus years, some of whom are featured here. My Purple People, who in many cases did not know that they were lovingly identified as such, have led me on a path of discovery that continues to this day. To those people from far apart countries who shared in such profound and loving experiences with me, I am profoundly grateful.

Three people in particular supported and cajoled me when I found it difficult to stay with the process, and to Ramanathan Revathi, Susan Geye, and Dr. Barbara Browne, I want to say thank you. Barbara and Susan, you brought order to my unruly words, making them so that I sometimes cried when I re-read them. Thank you. You helped distill the essence of my message. Revathi, who did not understand my work but believed in me and encouraged me, thank you for giving me a place to write in the vestibule of your peaceful, loving home in Chennai, India, and thank you for plying me with food and regular cups of tea. And, of course, thank you for letting me use your mosquito bat to fend off the only creatures whose love I so dearly wanted to reject! Thank you, Revathi, for forcing me to write when I would rather have explored your vibrant city.

This has been a challenging journey, this journey to the top of the parapet, and it is one I could not have made without the loving support of many friends: Joe and Eithne Ring who provided a safe harbor from "stormy seas" when I needed it most; Julie and Brendan Chambers, who gave me the use of their house in Mayo and doses of unceasing encouragement; Michael Hayden, who lovingly opened the doors to his home in Dublin; and Ann and John McDonnell in Los Angeles, who provided a beautiful environment in the sun and who tirelessly read and gave constructive feedback and love. You all have been the mortal arms of God for me.

An ex-colleague once questioned why I was "bothering" to write this section, saying, "Whoever reads those acknowledgments in a book?" These words are written for the friends who made this book possible, and this is my acknowledgment of their being the "spokes in my wheel."

Keep me in your prayers.

Love,

Kate

PREFACE

Were we but to realize that life is a simple journey with absolutely nothing to fear we could joyfully live the life we were created for.

Katherine Connon, the Skeptical Healer

*T*rue Stories of Healing through Divine intervention. First-aid for the Soul is a groundbreaking book. It chronicles the unlikely evolution of the author, Kate Connon, a lifelong skeptic, as she struggles with the decision to abandon her secure mainstream professional career, with all its perceived security, for a healing gift that even she does not fully comprehend. Initially stemming from a simple reflex technique that the author used to provide therapeutic touch to profoundly disabled clients, the gift gradually evolved into something much more powerful. Through Kate's gift, clients experience profound healing and a direct and very personal connection to a higher power. This process ultimately has the potential to transform their lives.

Healing Visions provides a revolutionary and urgently needed new perspective on the role that God can and does play in our lives, here and now. The transformations that occur in the book reveal a fresh and intimate look at a personal higher power who is present and available to us if we are open to receiving her or him. Kate, using a selection of her experiences with clients from across Europe, the United States, and India, illustrates how close we are to, and how unconditionally loved we are by, this divine power.

Whether we use the name God, Jesus, Mohammed, Krishna, Goddess Lakshmi, or Buddha matters not. The point is that God, or however we name that which cannot be named, is very much alive in our lives—loving us unconditionally, laughing with us, and holding us close in ways we can scarcely imagine. The Jesus who appears to so many of the people in this book is not dead or hanging forlornly from a cross. He is present and vibrant—a laughing Jesus, strong and full of life. He offers unconditional love and lasting healing to all who are open to receiving him.

In this book, Kate refers to this higher power as God and Jesus because the clients she features have named it so. In India, clients sometimes refer to the higher power as the "old man." Many of Kate's clients across the globe have reported seeing a single eye looking down upon them, or beings they name Sai Baba, Goddess Lakshmi, or Mohammed. Again, the name or guise does not matter. The supreme and all-seeing being is unnameable; names are simply guises individuals use to make the higher power familiar to their belief systems. Kate calls the higher power "God" and uses the male gender because it is simple and comfortable for her. The reader may, of course, substitute a preferred name whenever he encounters Kate's use of "God" or "him" to describe the higher power. However we choose to name the supreme loving being, it will be inadequate.

The accounts in *Healing Visions* are provocative and heartrending. They are true stories of ordinary people like us who rediscover that their higher power is a constant presence and source of comfort in their daily lives. They are stories of hope, healing, and peace.

As we reel from our worldwide recession, increasingly facing unemployment, loss of home, and damaged relationships, we discover that all that we had based our security on is vanishing before our eyes; the ground we have known is, like quicksand, shifting below our feet. Once a rare event, suicide is becoming pandemic. Young people are facing hopelessness. In many cases, those of us who should be looking into a safe retirement are faced with job loss, loss of pension, and loss of home. We have built our lives on collapsing structures and have depended on what we *own* for our security and sense of selves. Now, more than ever, the world needs to hear the stories in this book.

Topics covered in this book include abuse, forgiveness, life after death, and the acceptance of God's will. Whatever the magnitude of your suffering, to know a supreme being is with you unconditionally is such a blessing. This book, with its examination of universal issues, reinforces that blessing. Where appropriate, Kate offers practical visualization exercises and reflections to enable the reader's personal healing.

This is not a religious text, and it does not prescribe any religious doctrine. It simply allows the reader to consider new paths toward lasting healing of body, mind, and spirit. Through others' healing experiences, the reader may reach a deeper understanding of abuse, the call to forgiveness, life after death, God's will for us, and self-healing. It is not an exaggeration to say that every man, woman, and child should read this book. Across the globe and encompassing all doctrines, our higher power has many different names and facets, but his message is singular and universal: Each one of us is special. We are loved and supported by our higher power in every breathing moment.

This book says, "Wake up, everybody! God is alive in your life." God is not a "one day per week" God or an "I am in trouble" God. Jesus is not a name we use when we can't find our car keys and we're late for work. Unconditional love, compassion, and joy are all right here waiting for us to embrace. God is not sitting on a white cloud or on a twenty-two-karat gold throne waiting to judge us when we cease our lives' journeys. God is in every breath we breathe. God loves the perceived "good" and "bad" with equal passion, and most importantly, God is right beside and within you as you read these words. He is not a single breath away.

Dr John H Hicks MD paediatrician
Medical Director of Elementals Living, Delevan, Wisconsin. USA

INTRODUCTION: HEALING VISIONS

As human beings, our greatness lies not so much in being able to remake the world—that is the myth of the atomic age—as in being able to remake ourselves.

Mohandas Gandhi

If I had inadvertently picked this book off the bookshelf fifteen years ago, I would have quickly dismissed it as the work of a quack, hoped that no one had spotted me picking it up, and replaced it on the shelves posthaste. Not my cup of tea at all. My journey had only just commenced, and I was not ready.

I am a skeptic. And I am a healer. "Skeptical healer" may sound like a contradictory term, perhaps alien in the accepted language of healing, but there it is. After years of doubt, I have, and sometimes with great reluctance, been forced to accept that there is an active intelligent source, much greater I, working through me and connecting directly with my clients.

Over the years, I have heard appalling stories from clients regarding their experiences at the hands of con men and women who claimed to be healers. I am as skeptical about those healers' abilities as I used to be about my own, and I make no apologies. I have been skeptical of much of what has occurred with my clients, so much so that I could not acknowledge my own healing gift for many years. An early client, Carol (pseudonym), a grounded and levelheaded woman, said to me years ago that I should write a book. My reply was something to the effect of, "Sure! They would lock me up if I related some of the things that occurred during my work with clients." I asked her if she told many people about the amazing things that had occurred during and following our sessions together. She replied with an immediate and emphatic no. "And you want me to put my head on the block and write about it?" She was silent.

Ten years later, I am putting my head on the proverbial block, quite simply because now I feel I have no choice. You may read the detailed case histories with a certain skepticism; believe me, I initially recorded them with much more. A friend gave me the following feedback when he was shown my first, tentative pages: "Too much God in it. You will be aiming at a very small niche market. What you are writing is not commercial." He did not have one single constructive remark to make. I was dreadfully disappointed. Later, a prospective editor who read sample chapters asked me for three references from people who knew me before she would discuss working on the manuscript. Presumably she wished to ascertain my sanity! A few years before then, I would have packed up my laptop and mothballed my fledgling attempts. I write this book now because, despite my fears, I cannot *not* write it. My head is now well above that parapet of mainstream security I used to need, and I am ready to take the risk of being seen and perhaps judged. I am ready to honor the gift I have been blessed with.

The accounts you are about to read will, I have no doubt, challenge your belief system and perhaps my credibility. Many well-meaning people have suggested that the experiences as reported in the following case histories are the result of my clients' hopeful and overactive imaginations. I fully understand attempts to rationalize what I am unable to scientifically explain. I came from the same stable, so to speak, and shared the same doubt. I do not pretend to understand everything that happens during my treatment sessions. For that reason, I report my sessions with clients almost verbatim. You must make up your own mind.

I have the greatest respect for the clients featured in this book and am very grateful for having known them. I admit that, at times, I have fleetingly thought that their experiences in our sessions pushed the boundaries of credibility. My beliefs have been regularly challenged, and I have consistently questioned and doubted. I now, however, unquestionably accept that all those who appear in this book have experienced a deep and spiritually tangible connection to their higher power.

As a child, I was taught about a judgmental and wrathful God, a God I feared, and—particularly in the years following the early and painful death of my mother from cancer—a God I did not value. A good and loving God, I reasoned, would never take a mother away from her young family. I vividly remember my outraged responses when the priest at my mother's deathbed said to me, "There, there, Kate—it's God's will." My grief-stricken outburst of "D---- God! He's a B----" brought a shocked silence. Although I was then oblivious to his feelings, I suspect the priest regretted his ill-chosen words. I am thankful that twenty-four years later, ironically following the death of my father, I found a different God, a present God, a God of pure and unconditional love.

During the years following my father's death, I slowly became more interested in spirituality, but not in a Christian model. In fact, I felt antipathy toward the Christians' claim that God was theirs alone. In school, I had been taught that "only Catholics got to see heaven," and, horror of horrors, I was attracted to a Protestant boy at the nearby school!

During my first visit to India many years later, in 2004, I discovered that my favorite apostle, Saint Thomas, died outside Chennai (Madras) on the east coast of India. Throughout my personal journey, I had felt an affinity toward the forever doubting Thomas. I knew how he must have felt, needing concrete and measurable evidence of Jesus' resurrection. For that reason, I was drawn to visit the church on the hill at Chennai where he had preached and subsequently had been murdered. As I stood on the same sun-baked ground that Thomas had stood on over two thousand years earlier, I experienced with a shiver the sudden realization that he was once, as were the other followers of Jesus, flesh and blood. This realization felt quite strange. On that quiet hillside, for the first time in my life, Jesus and the apostles left mythology and became real human beings.

My first reaction to something unusual or different has usually been mistrust, skepticism. Even today, when I hear of some new therapy, I am wary. My doubting Thomas sits on my shoulder constantly, a wary beady-eyed bird that is ready to attack. Increasingly, people concoct, sell, and buy numerous miracle potions for various conditions. People are crying out for relief from the trauma of coping with today's fast, demanding lifestyle, a lifestyle that often results in escalating sickness rates from cancer, heart disease, and AIDS. Research carried out in the United States by The Robert Wood Johnson Foundation Commission to Build a Healthier America found that overall, during 2005–2007, 45.2 percent of adults aged 25 to 74 years reported being in less than very good health. This percentage varied across states, from 34.7 percent in Vermont to 52.9 percent in Mississippi. Even taking into consideration various contributing factors, such as education and income level, these are disturbing figures. Replicated across the globe, these figures reflect a sick world. The most widely prescribed drugs worldwide are for depression, followed closely by those for hypertension. We can schedule and finance moon trips, yet one in four deaths is from cancer, and we remain far from discovering any cure. Despite all sorts of advances in medicine and technology, people still regard their health as being poor today. Our affluence has not bought the one thing we rate most highly—our physical, emotional, and spiritual health.

A few years ago, at a client's request, I spent a week in Mexico. I was horrified at the untested and unregulated treatments meted out to terminally ill patients, who, in their desperate need to believe in a miracle, had lost their powers of discrimination. One man who was diagnosed with terminal cancer allowed the site of his cancer to be painted with a black tar-like substance because he was told it would heal him. He, as many do, returned home disillusioned and closer to death. In my local county, one woman was told by a "healer" to cease taking essential medicines. She subsequently had a fatal attack of asthma. People who are ill cling, as if on a life raft, to any vestige of hope. I wholeheartedly subscribe to the power of the placebo effect and acknowledge that our beliefs can and do heal. However, sadly, many new miracle cures are cons used to extract money from the ill. Just today, as I took a break from writing this introduction, my plumber related a story about a time when he was trying to save his critically ill son. He paid a huge sum of money, the equivalent of a month's salary, to a quack who has since been jailed. The quack had sold him arsenic.

While many of us now live longer, we still frequently and erroneously measure our quality of life in terms of material gains rather than happiness. Jeremy Bentham (1748–1832), the philosopher and father of utilitarianism, was seen as a radical when he attempted to theorize about happiness in his 1789 book, *Introduction to the Principles of Morals and Legislation*. It is interesting that over two hundred years later, governments worldwide now address the subject of happiness indexes. In the United Kingdom, politicians across the political spectrum agree with the old Beatles lyric, "Money can't buy me love … can't buy me love … no, no, no."

For this book, I have selected case histories that, I believe, will resonate with many readers. I have, given the fallibility of memory, reported as candidly as possible on the experiences my clients have had. In the interest of confidentiality, I have used pseudonyms. I share my journey and that of my clients with you so that you may benefit from the experiences and healing we have shared. For those of you who are not personally touched by these sometimes amazing and often moving experiences, I sincerely wish that reading these accounts results in an opening of your hearts and minds to the great and interconnected beings we all are and to the possibility of a higher being or loving intelligence who is present in each of our lives. My hope is that should a particular experience touch you, you might use an appropriate exercise from this book in meditation. As you read this book, I encourage you to have your own healthy skeptic, your own doubting Thomas, in tow. The experiences I have witnessed have gone into battle with my own skepticism over the years, so take in and digest what is good for you and what you are ready for. Disregard the rest. You may perhaps return to the rest at some later stage.

ONE GOD MANY FACES

Neil Hague is the credit for the illustration

ONE: FROM SKEPTIC TO HEALER

He who would learn to fly one day must first learn to stand and walk and run and climb and dance; one cannot fly into flying.

Friedrich Nietzsche

My introduction to complementary healing therapies came in 1988, when I was managing services for learning disabled adults in Larne, Northern Ireland. I had been working with the disabled population since 1980 in a variety of posts, but this was one of the most rewarding jobs thus far.

In my position, I managed a handpicked and highly motivated staff of approximately forty people. All were a pleasure to work with, from the two cleaners who teased and tormented me continually—Martha often leaving cheeky notes on my office desk to greet me in the mornings—to the dedicated day care workers and experienced social workers who made my job so easy. I had a truly dedicated, multidisciplinary team behind me that was keen to implement our individual programs. I confidently oversaw the planning and coordination of activities, such as assessment, literacy skills, work placements, personal safety, artistic development, and parent and caregiver reviews. These activities were all designed to maximize the life skills and independence of those in my care.

My learning disabled adults taught me so much. Uninhibited by social norms, they gave and received love without hesitation or game playing. Unfortunately, we would often have to design behavior programs to teach the most naive to be more restrained and socially correct. It saddened me that the real world was often too harsh and confrontational for the truly innocent of heart. I remember one parent, concerned for his vulnerable daughter's safety, telling me sadly, "I wish my daughter was not so attractive." Thankfully, there were many triumphs. One beautiful memory I hold dear is of a previously institutionalized, uncommunicative, and sullen young man's transformation into a confident person who could independently hop on the bus and travel to the gym for a workout. Many of my clients were severely disabled, with multiple handicaps—some of them were blind, some deaf, and some without speech. In my quest for new therapeutic approaches to support them, I became interested in holistic health and wellness treatments, including sensory, hands-on approaches.

In 1988, at a health and social services conference in Blackpool, England, I received the name of a massage therapist based in London who was reputedly doing excellent work with people who were similarly learning disabled. Impressed by the woman's credentials, I immediately decided to bring her over to Ireland to train my staff. I felt my members and staff would benefit. Thankfully, the local charity, *Mencap*, agreed to finance it, and my director of social services, the late Pat McHugh, sanctioned it. Therapeutic touch was important to the well-being of those under our care, and it was central, of course, to the therapist's practice. Although the adults under our care benefited from formal physiotherapy sessions, touch in physiotherapy was incidental rather than intentional, and these sessions were always budget-restricted.

Two months after receiving approval, my entire staff team of cooks, drivers, social workers, support staff, and I underwent two days of serious instruction that was enlivened by fun and laughter. During this instruction, we developed a hands-on awareness of the importance of caring touch. We converted the dining room to a massage room and improvised using the dining tables as makeshift massage tables. The masseuse took the entire team through the basics of massage. We were given enough for us to appreciate the feel-good factor and to experience examples of safe and simple practices.

The trainer also introduced us briefly to reflexology. When she pressed what I subsequently realized to be the reflex point to the sinus on one woman's foot, I was utterly amazed to see the immediate effect it had opening the woman's nasal passage. How she could seemingly diagnose and treat illness and disorders through a person's foot amazed even the skeptic in me, and right there I was hooked. In fact, I was smitten by everything I experienced over those two days.

A week later, when an advertisement appeared in the local church bulletin for part-time training in reflexology, I decided to apply. There was one problem, however: I did not have the prescribed fee. The fee did not amount to a vast investment, but in those days I was consistently living on the dangerous border of a large overdraft. Inwardly, I bargained that if the trainers would accept my fee in installments, I would do the training. They agreed to teach me, and for the next year I spent every chance I had working and learning about the anatomy, physiology, and meridians of the body. While my friends were reading light fiction on the beach that summer, I, who had never been a studious learner, was struggling to come to grips with metatarsal bones and kidneys.

After becoming licensed in reflexology in 1989, I was disappointed when my director refused to allow me to start a practice. He assured me that it was nothing personal—and, in fact, he later became a client of mine—but because abuse cases had started to surface in Northern Ireland, he felt it unwise to risk potential accusations. The newspapers were then full of allegations against staff in other establishments, and he felt that the hands-on approach we wished to take could be open to misinterpretation. It is interesting to note that the vast majority of care establishments now offer these types of hands-on therapies. In 1989, however, it was not to be. Rather than let my yearlong training go to waste, I started to work out of my home in Belfast, Northern Ireland. I began with friends and then, gradually, with strangers who had heard about me through referrals. Over the next few years, my home-based practice was small but steady. That changed in 1996, when a treatment experience shocked me into realizing that something new and powerful was starting to happen.

Reflexology is based on the principle that every organ in the body has a corresponding reflex point in the feet, hands, and ears. I was taught to slowly and meticulously stimulate each reflex point to effect change in the corresponding organs. Indeed, many clients received healing benefits after a number of reflexology sessions.

One Sunday I found myself, with great reluctance, treating a young man who had broken his collarbone in two places while playing rugby. He was awaiting an operation. I say "with reluctance," because when he telephoned for an appointment, I told him that I believed reflexology could not repair broken bones. He was adamant, however, and said that the pain, unresponsive to painkillers, was making him suicidal. With many misgivings, I agreed to see him.

When he stepped into my treatment room a few hours later, I could see he was struggling to hold back tears and observed beads of perspiration gathering on his creased brow. The pain in his shoulder was obviously excruciating. Gingerly protecting his smashed collarbone, he painstakingly lowered his large frame into the couch. Every one of his painful movements made me feel squeamish. No longer the strong, strapping thirty-year-old teacher of grammar school athletes, he had become a small vulnerable child about to cry.

I started to work, hoping that I could bring him some relief. He was silent for most of the session, but in the later stages of his treatment, he suddenly and quite abruptly asked, "What are you doing?" Assuming he was referring to my specific actions at that time I started to explain, only to be sharply interrupted by his exclamation "But I feel your hands inside my shoulder, putting my bones together!" I did not know how to respond. My two hands were firmly on his left foot, not inside his shoulder. What happened after that is unclear, as I was even more shocked than he. I had no explanation for what he had described. When I finished, he left my treatment room smiling broadly, unquestioningly looking ten years younger. I was left with many questions and no answers. This outcome was most definitely not a result of reflexology.

Two weeks later, the friend who had referred this young man to me told me that he had returned to his teaching post, healed of his break and without need for an operation. Amazed, I excitedly told a close friend what had happened. What a big mistake. What occurred next was disturbing: I was invited to my friend's home a few days later, only to be faced with a line of people who had heard the story and were now waiting for me to perform a "miracle." I felt sick to my stomach. I was not a healer and certainly not a miracle worker! What had happened was unusual— yes, even verging on the miraculous—but it was new and inexplicable to me. I was overwhelmed by the demand to "perform" and wanted to just run away. As soon as I could escape, I did. Although my friend was upset, I was still coming to terms with what had occurred during my session with the teacher and could not deal with the expectations he had thrust upon me.

For a month, I did not do many sessions. But slowly, at the request of clients, I cautiously resumed my practice. Over the next few weeks, my left hand started causing me discomfort and pain. Eventually I saw my regular doctor, who diagnosed me with carpal tunnel syndrome, a condition in which the wrist bones constrict the vessels and cause numbness in the fingers. He advised rest while I awaited an operation to relieve the pressure on my wrist. I was horrified at the thought of surgery; I was concerned that it would be the end of my practice. Reflexology required strength in my fingers, something I was quickly losing. To support my wrist, the doctor prescribed a type of wrist sling, a contraption that made working with my hands out of the question.

During this period, I had begun a five-year training program in gestalt psychotherapy, an existential and experiential form of therapy developed by Fritz Perls and Paul Goodman in the 1950s. The approach emphasizes personal responsibility, focusing upon the individual's experience in the present moment, the therapist-client relationship, the environmental and social contexts of a person's life, and the self-regulating adjustments people make as a result of their overall situations. I worked with a group of accredited Scottish trainers. One weekend, I was providing a bed and meals for one of the training assistants. I told him about my wrist and the proposed surgery. Intuitively he responded, "Maybe you are meant to find another way to work." He further suggested that I attempt to work on his damaged knee by using the palms of my hands. Treating the whole thing as a bit of a joke, and with much more than my usual doubt, I agreed. To my surprise, he said that he felt intense heat coming from my hands and relief in his painful knee joint.

Uncomfortable with this new way of working, I dismissed the experience and his suggestion. A week later, I saw a cranial osteopath, who advised me that I did not have carpal tunnel syndrome at all; I actually had pinched nerves in my neck. He gently manipulated my cranial bones, and within forty-eight hours, my symptoms had evaporated. So much for the need for an operation! Thankfully, almost fifteen years later, I still haven't been contacted to schedule my surgery.

Nonetheless, the entire incident made me realize that perhaps I did need to re-examine my views on unorthodox healing methods. This new way of working meant change, and I had no textbook theory to support it. I was yet again reminded of how much I feared change. Though I was uncomfortable with the inexplicable, I realized that the brief period when I could not practice reflexology was providing me with some kind of signal. What the signal meant, I did not know. The theory that everything happens for a reason is all very well, but sometimes it is very difficult to make constructive use of an experience without accompanying awareness and insight. The incident did stimulate a broadening of my approach to the whole mechanics of healing, which I would soon put to good use.

A few weeks later, I was surprised when Joe, one of my first and regular reflexology clients, called to make an appointment for the day before he was getting married for the second time. Knowing his painful history, I suspected, though he never confirmed it, that he was feeling anxious about embarking on another marriage. In the early days of our working relationship, Joe challenged me mercilessly, bombarding me with questions on reflexology theory and practice. I often wondered why he even bothered to receive treatments so regularly! Later, he admitted that he did this in order to seek reassurance that he could fully trust me. He certainly kept me on my toes, whatever his motives.

On the day of this reflexology treatment, he complained of an increasingly painful left upper arm during the session. I had never worked with a client above the ankle before, but for some then unknown reason I asked Joe if I could hold his upper arm in my hands. He immediately agreed. As I held his arm gently, I watched, awed, as this outwardly unemotional, confident, mind-mannered businessman shed silent tears. They started with a trickle and then ran unabated down his cheeks. I did not speak, as in all honesty, I did not know what to say. Although he had been a challenging client, I had grown very fond of Joe. His tears concerned me. I wondered if he was having second thoughts on the eve of his marriage. If so, what a time to have them! And more importantly, how could I help him?

When he regained his composure, Joe told me that during the time I was holding his arm, he saw a vision of his deceased mother in a setting he remembered as a child. The vision of his mother had brought him a lot of comfort and reassurance. She was smiling at him and somehow managed to convey to Joe that she was happy for him and approved of his upcoming marriage.

Some time later, Joe told me that following his treatment, he had taken his marriage vows as a more emotionally centered person. I could not have wished for a better wedding present for him.

For some reason, this incident, however unusual, did not shock me. Because I knew Joe so well and valued his levelheaded approach, his unquestioning acceptance seemed to ease my fears about the highly unusual turn of events, and it also made me aware that I had bracketed many previous experiences, such as the teacher with the broken collarbone, as mere coincidence or chance. I consistently dismissed what I could not rationalize. Slowly things were slipping past my skeptical filter.

While all this was slowly developing, I was promoted. Instead of managing day services, I would now be training and assessing social workers. My new job involved a great deal of developmental work, as I'd be setting UK-wide standards—national vocational qualifications (NVQs)—across the care spectrum, work which was both rewarding and exciting. The position appeared ideal, one that challenged and widened my horizons. With a private, spacious office overlooking green fields and a dedicated personal secretary, Brenda I was encouraged and supported to carry out the types of training programs that I enjoyed. Much of my new assignment involved supervising social work students as their practice teacher, for which I traveled countrywide. At the same time, I was carrying out joint training with the police service and voluntary organizations. Given a great deal of autonomy, I could choose subjects I felt particularly drawn to for training and developmental courses. To my delight, I could also work flexible hours, which included writing reports from home. I had a job and salary that many would view with envy. A whole new world was opening up for me.

In truth, what neither my new colleagues nor the ones I left behind in Larne knew was that behind the closed doors of my lovely, spacious office with its views over the countryside, my tears silently flowed on many a lonely afternoon. How I missed my learning disabled clients! Suddenly there was no one telling me how great I was, no one to give me the spontaneous loving hug. I was thrust into an emotionally lonely place. My first student, who worked with older people in residential care, in fact, sharply demanded, "How are you qualified to assess me?" She had obviously done her homework on my career. For years, my background had been working with learning disabled adults, but not older people. It was that she was challenging me, not the content of her question, which startled me. I responded with outward calmness, "A social worker utilizes the same skills whatever the context. You are not undergoing training to work with older clients exclusively." Below my professional, outwardly calm response, however, my heart was racing and my inner thoughts were in turmoil. Oh, if only she had known how anxious, how unsure I was now that I was faced with this stark, new, fast-moving assessment world. The admiration and respect I had become accustomed to in my former easygoing environment was gone like a puff of smoke. I had become the proverbial little fish in a big and alien pond.

Ironically, my unexpectedly painful promotion was to be the best thing that ever happened to me. It caused me to take the first step toward major change in my life. Because I could no longer depend on others to reflect how good I felt about myself, I had to learn practically from scratch (or so it felt then) to love and appreciate myself. The steady fix of affirmations I had received from my clients, caregivers, and staff had vanished. I was forced to leave my emotional crutches behind.

This was the beginning of my interest in personal development. My journey led me to attend many self-development workshops, notably a number of visits to the late Eileen Caddy's Findhorn Foundation in the north of Scotland. On one occasion at Findhorn, I attended a workshop by Caroline Myss. Caroline, the international bestselling author of many books, is an amazing medical clairvoyant who can see not only a person's illness, but also the trauma and emotional history that caused the illness in the first place. Now I could more fully understand and rationalize the experiences of some of my former clients: my friend Joe, the Gestalt training assistant, the young man with the broken collarbone, and many more seeming miracles I had previously dismissed because of my lack of comprehension.

Another healer who had an influence on my developing awareness and practice was Clyde Ford, who wrote *Where Healing Waters Meet*. Clyde Ford was a great source of support. I experienced many *Aha*! moments while reading this simple but powerful book about how trauma could get caught and stored in the body. Immediately, I connected these lessons to the inexplicable experiences my clients were having in my home-based reflexology practice.

By 1990, I had decided to pursue a master's degree in Gestalt psychotherapy training. I found that my developing awareness through Gestalt enriched the work I was doing within both the social services training department and my growing reflexology practice. At the same time, the workload in the training department was becoming much heavier. I was involved in a lot of developmental work, traveling back and forth across the UK as new care standards were developed and tested. At the same time, following a radio interview in Belfast during which the interviewer presented a glowing picture of my work, my reflexology practice was attracting new clients.

The stress of trying to maintain my commitment to two jobs and additional training was taking a toll on my energy and health. Finally, increasingly drawn to my healing work, I requested part-time employment in order to do justice to both. The new assistant director of training refused, saying that my post was too specialized to find a suitable replacement.

Shortly after my request was turned down, however, I noticed that my clients were starting to have more and more powerful responses to my developing process. Simultaneously, I was moving further and further away from the standard practice of reflexology into some new level of healing. A client's history started to take on a new significance. I began to realize that somewhere in the depths of their pasts lay the roots of all their current diseases.

Over the following months, the changes continued. I am not sure at what point I stopped practicing formal reflexology altogether and started to follow my intuition. The change was so subtle and incremental that I did not become anxious or feel out of my depth, as I had before.

These changes and my new calmness were epitomized by my series of treatments with Jane, a reporter who had broken her back in a helicopter accident. Jane came to see me a year after her nearly fatal crash. Despite months of physiotherapy, she remained in almost constant pain. As with many of my clients, it took several sessions for her to relax fully during the treatment process. During one session, however, while in a deeply relaxed state, she unexpectedly started to recount and relive the experience of the crash. The crash scene unfolded like a series of slides. Vividly she described frame after frame—sitting in the copter immediately following the crash, listening to the doctor in the hospital say to someone that she may not survive, and then listening to him say to yet another that she may never walk again. The extremely traumatic images came bursting forth, and with them came healing from the pain and trauma she had been carrying since the accident. As she relived the scenes, her body quivered and shook as if she were experiencing a minor seizure. As she shook, I realized that she was exorcising the memory from her very cells.

Throughout this process, I was holding Jane's feet very gently in my hands, but I was not manipulating them. Jane's healing came not from reflexology, but through my, as yet inexplicable, connection with her.

As time went on, I felt increasingly right modifying the actions I carried out during a session. I would begin as usual, manipulating the client's large toe and ankle. Somehow, and to this day I do not understand it, that connection initiates a flow of energy throughout the client's body, supporting her journey to a higher level of consciousness. There was no quiet voice—or, for that matter, a booming one—telling me what to do or how to proceed, just a deep, inexplicable knowing, which did not stem from cognition, that what I was now doing was right.

Unlike the theory of reflexology, in which the energy flow directly correlates with the meridians flowing horizontally through the body, the energy flow I was now observing could be felt throughout the body and was experienced differently from client to client. In one client, it would feel like a tingle; another would experience a sensation of pins and needles, weightlessness, or heaviness; yet another, waves. Each client had his own unique experience.

My Purple People

As my clients had stronger and more unusual reactions, I generally took their reactions in stride. However, when a client would first detail unusual physical or visual sensations, I would fall back on "Ms. Skeptic," assuming my client was imagining them. Then a pattern would seem to appear—suddenly, a second client and then a third would describe a similar phenomenon. Clients would describe sensations in which parts or all of their bodies felt as though they weren't there or as though they were tilted on the couch or, more unusually, as though individual body parts were turning, anatomically impossibly, as though on a spit.

Because I was treating sane, sensible, and mostly professional adults, I could no longer ascribe these responses to their imaginations. I was gradually forced to accept that, once again, something inexplicable was happening. The common denominator with this distinct group of clients was that they all, without exception, mentioned seeing the color purple during their treatments. These clients were not particularly imaginative or given to fantasy. Because I had high regard for their objectivity and maturity, I could not dismiss their collective experiences. With the greatest of respect, I nicknamed them my "Purple People."

One of my Purple People, Ann, who was later to support me in making enormous changes in my life, reported a particularly unusual and notable occurrence. Ann was in her early fifties and ran a training department in a global organization. We first met through my capacity as a social work trainer, sharing student assessment panels at conferences. A committed Christian, Ann, despite much personal tragedy and suffering, had a faith I envied; she was always a beautiful and gracious person to work with. Ann came to me seeking relief from lower back pain, a sacroiliac problem that stemmed from the birth of her daughter some twenty years previously. During early sessions, Ann had the sensation that her body was tilted on my treatment couch and that sections of her body were turning as if on a spit. She would describe her entire left side rotating, which made no anatomical sense whatsoever, but I had become so familiar with these phenomena that it then appeared commonplace.

On one occasion, however, Ann described a sudden and intense pain in her sacroiliac, as if some external force were pushing her hipbones back into shape. Sharp and intense, her pain was becoming almost unbearable; then it gradually lessened; and finally, it abated. Ann's description of this experience of acute pain subsiding was not unusual; it had become the norm with my Purple People. I surmised that this was part of the healing process, as energy blocks were clearing.

However, on Ann's return visit, she reported a very unusual happening. The previous Sunday at church, as she had stood up for part of the service, she had had an agonizing pain in the same area. She said that it felt as if unseen hands were pushing her pelvis back into the correct position from behind. The sensation was similar to what she had experienced during my treatment. Ann's chronic back pain ceased following our work together, but when I recently approached her for her permission to use an excerpt from our sessions for my book, she told me that she still, to this day, has the same feeling of someone pushing in her hip bones when she is having a particularly spiritual experience.

Ann is a very special woman and friend to whom I shall always be grateful for coming into my life. I value all my clients without exception, but I found Ann and the others in this group of people particularly fascinating. They were, in the main, business people for whom these types of occurrences were unusual. But they all, without exception, were not alarmed by them. If the same things happened to me, I reasoned, I would politely thank my therapist and never again expose myself to such seemingly freakish happenings.

One thing I found particularly amazing is that my Purple People were connecting on a much higher level of consciousness in such a matter-of-fact way. These clients calmly interacted with the here and now of their experiences, which, in turn, enabled me to equally calmly accept how my work was evolving. I started to have more confidence and faith in what was happening. Change was occurring incrementally at a pace I no longer feared. However, I was not aware that more challenging experiences were just around the corner.

Another one of my clients powerfully reinforced my growing awareness that patterns can occur in people's lives when there are unresolved lessons to be learned. Deirdre was a highly respected manager of a large accounting firm and came to me following her second suicide attempt. Her husband had heard my radio interview and had pleaded with her to make an appointment. Her story was remarkable. Although at the pinnacle of her career, and in demand all over Europe, she felt immobilized and bullied by a junior male member of her staff. Her exaggerated response to what appeared, at least on the face of it, to be a non-threatening situation, did not make rational sense. She was his senior in age and status. My evolving healing practice then comprised my adapted reflexology and Gestalt counseling, and it took me many sessions to unravel that Deirdre had a pattern of this happening in her history. The individuals were different, but the theme remained the same: a junior male member of her staff continually bullied her. On each occasion, her response was to change jobs, and following two of these occasions, she attempted suicide. This response was totally disproportionate to the events she related.

With delicate probing, we uncovered that she had had an early childhood experience when she was subjected to vicious and sustained bullying by a neighbor the same age as the men who bullied her as an adult. Instinctively, I knew that unless she stood up to the current bully, she would continually repeat history over and over. She had to learn to address the early childhood issue in order to stop its repetition in her adult life. I was convinced that until she did, she would unconsciously seek out perceived bullies to repeat the debilitating pattern. I wish I could say that she stood up to the man at work. I would love to give readers a happy ending. Following our last meeting together, Deirdre did what she had done so many times before: she applied for, and, of course, got another position. When I discussed this with her, she replied, "I know, I know, Kate, but this time I am doing it with awareness!" I had to respect her right to self-determination. She was at least armed with the awareness of the pattern in her life and was a step closer to actively choosing healing. This was during my own transition period in my career, and I did not hear from Deirdre again. I hope she succeeded in ending the cycle of bullying and abuse by standing up for herself once and for all.

As the months went on, I again requested part-time work and, again, this was refused. As before, the mere request to go part-time somehow signaled to my spiritual guides that I was committed to the healing work and, again, my clients' experiences intensified. I suddenly connected the two and realized that the more committed I became to the healing work, the more my clients and I received. Many healers report that their clients were, and are, their teachers. My experience was similar. I grew as they grew.

At last, another of my work colleagues was granted part-time work, setting a precedent. My assistant director could no longer refuse; I got my wish and was granted part-time work for one year. 1999 was a surprising year for many reasons, but on a purely mundane level, I now had to exist on less than half my salary. As I previously mentioned, I was always in debt. My overdraft facility of two thousand pounds was never overstepped, but for five or six years I could not pay it off. Illogically, at the end of those first six months of living on half my income, I was no worse off than when I had been working full-time. During that same period, I also spent three weeks in the south of France and three weeks in California. I did not earn any more money, but somehow I had enough. I received no additional income during this period, yet my overdraft facility at the end of that period was constant. It was incomprehensible.

At the end of that year, I decided to leave my job. Although I had come to love my work, I knew I needed to move on. Unnerved about this pending change, however, I started having recurring nightmares, which I referred to as my "high ledge dreams." In these dreams, I would be on a ledge. It could be the edge of a building or a wall, but it was always some kind of precipice. On each occasion, I would reach a chasm that would prevent me from moving forward. No matter how I explored the chasm, I could not cross it.

In the safe light of day, the dreams did not seem frightening in the least, but at night, I would sometimes wake up perspiring, feeling panicked and terrified. Having no idea what they meant, I felt out of control. I engaged a therapist and discussed my dreams with him. Week after week, I related my different dreams. The situations were always different, but the theme remained the same. Fascinated, he practically hijacked my dreams, but he did not solve the riddle.

One night, I had the same dream, but this time it had a different ending. I was walking along the edge of a cliff and came, yet again, to the now familiar chasm. I knew I had to get to the other side, but the drop was deep and sheer. Below me lay the rough sea, and in the middle, far below, a tiny patch of green. As I gazed into the abyss, I spotted a friend, Tina, swimming in the water. She was smiling and beckoning for me to join her. The water suddenly appeared calm. She looked so comfortable, confident, and happy.

13

I did not dive in, but the next morning the meaning of the dream became clear to me. Tina, who had been swimming in the sea in my dream, had risked giving up full-time employment and was successfully working as an independent organizational trainer. It was simple. The various chasms were symbolic of my fear of change, and somehow seeing Tina so free and happy gave me courage to step into the unknown. I never had the high ledge dream again. I also immediately saved my weekly therapy bill!

Jesus

Raised a Roman Catholic, I spent much of my youth "knowing" God as a somewhat distant judge whom, if I were fortunate, I would meet someday when I died. Based on my early teachings and personal experience, I saw no reason to believe that if there were a God at all, he was kind and loving.

As for Jesus, I admit that I have said his name in anger, frustration, and shock. I have exclaimed his name many times and for many inappropriate reasons, and admittedly, I seldom used to say it with thanks or prayer. I have to confess that until experiences with clients taught me differently, Jesus did not feature strongly in my life, despite much encouragement from two good role models and devotees, Ronny Kelly and Gerald Harris. If anything, because I did not wish to be labeled Catholic or even Christian, I acknowledged Jesus simply as another holy prophet.

In 2000, during the period when I was still having the recurring nightmares and preparing to leave my comfortable job, friends, and home in Belfast, I was treating Róisín, a businesswoman in her early thirties. I had known Róisín for years. Like me, she was not religious and was, in fact, agnostic. She was one of my Purple People, and I always enjoyed working with her. She was an interesting woman to know, and each session was a wonderful journey that encompassed all her senses.

During one particular session that started out in a normal fashion, Róisín remarked, "Kate, I see you … you have a halo around your head … you are glowing." This was new, a change from our "usual" experience. I bracketed her words off, but not before I allowed myself a brief smile at her unfamiliar view of me, and I continued to gently manipulate her ankle in a clockwise direction. We were about half an hour into the work when she suddenly bolted upright on my couch. Her eyes seemed to be staring at me and yet not seeing me at the same time. Her glazed expression first startled and then alarmed me.

Although I was becoming unnerved, I said, in what I hoped was a calm voice, "What's wrong Róisín?" I wished to reassure her and, in doing so, myself. I realized I was holding my breath, and it seemed like an eternity before she answered. As I waited, I became more and more anxious. Tears started flowing down her drawn face, and she seemed to be struggling to speak, as her mouth silently opened and closed.

Finally, she said, almost calmly, "I saw Jesus … I saw Jesus."

What could I say? Here I was, someone who barely acknowledged Jesus, hearing these words from Róisín, an agnostic. My old friend, Ms. Skeptic, never too far away, stepped in to my rescue. As I became composed, I questioned, "What did he look like?" I suppose I half-expected and desired to hear her describe the thorns on the head image, which I abhor, and which would have reassured me that this stereotypical image of Christ on the cross was simply her imagination.

Instead she replied, "He was smiling at me."

"How do you know it was Jesus?"

She did not reply to that. Instead she lay down again with a short but mirthless laugh and said, "Now try to follow that one, Kate."

With more than a passing unease, I continued to manipulate her feet. Róisín had seen something—of that, I had absolutely no doubt whatsoever—but Jesus smiling at her was too much for me to swallow. I dismissed it, just as I had done so many times before. I again relaxed into my routine until Róisín remarked, "I see a field of lovely white flowers."

Nothing unusual about that, I thought. *Thank God.* As she reported this new vision, she sounded calm and looked relaxed. Then she said, "I see a vortex coming toward me."

Again, I was not surprised at her revelation; it was not too unusual coming from one of my Purple People. Then, again suddenly, she sprung upright like a jack-in-the box, with the same unnerving expression as before. This time, however, I was even more worried, as her deathly white face looked visibly shocked. My breath seemed to catch in my throat. Totally out of my depth, I struggled to find words, but none would come. Eventually, she talked through her tears, "I saw the Holy Spirit … I see a heart over my head with a huge red light pouring out from it … it's the sacred heart. Kate, am I going to die?"

Stunned, I attempted to comfort her, but I had no reassurance to offer. I could not make sense of the association she made between what she reported seeing and death. To be honest, I was as shaken as she was, and I remember little else of this day. I do remember that then, in what seemed like a flash, Róisín left my treatment room, leaving me dazed by what had occurred. Saint Thomas, my skeptical archetype, was nowhere around to reassure me. I had to face the fact that something extremely powerful had just occurred, and I could not ignore, rationalize, or simply dismiss it.

I could not get Róisín's vision of Jesus out of my head. The next day, I postponed appointments and avoided going into my treatment room. I was wary of going back there alone, as I was in awe of the place where our experience had occurred. Suddenly, the room had become a sacred place; a place I felt I no longer belonged. I did not want to be reminded of Róisín's vision, unnerved by any meaning I could attribute to it; I wanted to forget what had happened.

Fortunately, another one of my Purple People, Ann, with her well-grounded and unshakable faith—and who belonged to a religious order—was due to attend for an appointment two days later. On the pretext of forewarning her, should a similar experience occur, I telephoned her and, while maintaining confidentiality, related my session with Róisín. In truth, I called Ann because at that moment in my life the tables were turned. I was the one who needed support.

Strangely, Ann seemed unconcerned, reminding me that I had told her the previous week that I had prayed for some sign that I was right in giving up my job and home to focus on my healing work. I had completely forgotten that I had indeed asked for some kind of sign. Ann's view was that I had also received a message in what Róisín had seen; perhaps Róisín's visions were meant even more for me, she suggested. Taken aback by her response, I said that I felt I was not "holy" enough to deal with this kind of thing. Again, Ann with her lovely simple wisdom said, "The Lord will only give you what he knows you can carry. Kate. Just trust in the Lord."

Not quite believing her words, I was nevertheless moved and somewhat reassured by them. Little did I know that Jesus, as healer, was soon to be brought in from the cold mythology and dusty realms of my distant faith to become significant and ever-present in my healing practice.

The following day, Ann came for her treatment and had what was for her a perfectly "normal" session. I was very relieved! A few days later, I spoke to Róisín. She told me that when she recounted her session to Mike, her husband, he told her that he envied her the experience. Shortly after this, and prior to leaving to spend a year in the United States, I again treated Róisín. I do not know whether I was relieved or saddened that her treatment was without a similar incident.

When I contacted Róisín—which is her real name, as she requested—for permission to use her experience, she reminded me that in our last session she had looked at me at one point and had seen a halo-like light around my head. I had dismissed her vision because I was struggling, then as now, to accept my portrayal as a holy person. She wrote to me about her session with Jesus, saying, "As unnerving as this experience was, it was beautiful, Kate."

On July 6, 2000, as soon as I awoke, I went to my computer and, giving three months notice, penned my resignation. That action felt like some important ritual, delineating a new beginning in my life. Without any trace of anxiety or fear, I was fully committed to my healing work. Within three months, I had cleared my desk, sold my home in Belfast, bought a home in Westport, and said my goodbyes to colleagues and friends. The one concession I made to my fear of this huge change was to remove the nameplate that read "Assistant Principal Social Worker" from my office door and take it home. It was irrational, I knew, but my nameplate somehow symbolized the identity and safe status I was leaving behind. My ego, reminiscent of a child's security blanket, needed something to hold onto.

The London School of Gestalt had offered me the opportunity to complete a master's degree in Gestalt Psychotherapy, but I decided against it. All my life, I had conformed to the values instilled by my parents and others. My need for a secure, respectable career had been paramount until now. Something in me rebelled against further routine. Instead, I packed my bags and left Belfast for my late-onset gap year, which is the term used to describe the period usually taken by students before college. I went abroad. In that year, my practice gradually but radically changed from reflexology to the total acceptance of my as yet undefined healing gift.

In the spring of 2001, I returned to Ireland and set up a practice in Westport, County Mayo. I had visited Achill, County Mayo in 1999, and I had fallen in love with this county where my mother had been born and brought up. I felt I was returning home. For the following two years, I spent winters in Spain and summers in Westport. Again, I had the best of both worlds.

In 2003, while on a visit to Belfast, I was interviewed by a newspaper reporter. In her presence I had treated a friend of hers, and, following this meeting, she wrote a very flattering article about my work. This brought more people to my practice. By this time, I had abandoned calling myself a reflexologist and tentatively told people when they asked what I did, "I am a healer."

TWO: THE HEALING PROCESS

Our sorrows and wounds are healed only when we touch them with compassion.

Buddha

Since my foray into healing therapies in 1988, my gift has evolved so gently and incrementally that I sometimes find it difficult to pinpoint when major changes occurred. After leaving my formal reflexology training behind, I searched fruitlessly for a term to describe what was then the unknown force guiding me toward my new method of working with clients. I had a strong need to name it and thus possibly understand and explain it to others. Not fitting in with any recognized practice disturbed me. Many terms came to mind as I searched for the right fit. Finally, I had to admit and accept that I just did not know beyond the truth that my work was and is a knowing, a simple knowing.

My clients' healing experiences were increasingly so unusual and complex that I was required to pay a great deal more attention to my method of recording sessions. The changes I witnessed were at times dramatic and instant. One man, as I gently rotated his large toe, suddenly felt and heard a loud crack in his cervical vertebra. Initially frightened by what occurred, he was delighted to quickly discover that mobility had returned to his previously stiff neck in an instant. Clinical depression would decrease very quickly on many occasions, and for some it even seemed to disappear after one session. For purposes of careful monitoring and certification, I started to meticulously write down clients' responses from each physical movement or manipulation. Every one of my rotations and stretching actions seemed to have a clearly defined response that varied from person to person and would manifest in any part of the bodily energy system not functioning at its optimum level.

To this day, each client's experience during a session is unique. For example, three people may ostensibly have a heart issue. Whatever the underlying cause is , it's all the same. One may feel a pronounced awareness of her heart warmly beating faster while I manipulate her feet, while another may feel a weight pressing down on his chest area. And, a third may experience the sensation of a band tightening around her chest as I work. Still other clients maintain that the heart organ seems larger and stronger as I work. All of these experiences are part of the healing process, and all are different. On occasion, despite an apparent heart difficulty, a few, for an unknown reason, will have no direct awareness of their hearts. Each client is unique, and each reports a unique response to the work.

By 2001, for this very reason, I had a growing awareness of the importance of extensively documenting my work. I was vainly trying to form a workable hypothesis and, thus, a rational theoretical framework. Working with the inexplicable was a struggle when I had such a need to understand.

In response to clients in the past, I endeavored to teach my clients my process by taking them through my actions. Unfortunately for them, their results when they tried to emulate these actions did not correlate with my own. To the casual observer, what I do during a treatment appears routine, even laughably simplistic. Commencing with the right foot, I first stretch the foot gently. Then I rotate the large toes and the heels, coupled with some very light and soothing fingertip motions across the metatarsals of the foot. That's it. It's so basic and easy. I have no straightforward textbook theory as to why the movements stimulate the responses they do. What occurs when I carry out those motions is totally out of my control. As I repeatedly tell my clients, "I rotate your toes; the rest is up to God."

To understand what is happening during a treatment, visualize the bodily system as you would a river. When the river has no obstructions, it sparkles, full of vibrant life, and flows freely. However, if logs and debris jam up the river, the flow gradually slows down, and the river becomes stagnated in parts. The human energy system undergoes a similar process. Sustained stress from fearful thoughts, one's environment, trauma, and unhealthy behavior cause the flow of energy in the body to become blocked, become toxic. Left untreated, these blocks can lead to physical imbalances and chronic illness, such as hypertension, diabetes, and arthritis.

As I work with clients to clear these blocks, they identify various sensations. This does not necessarily indicate the presence of disease, but it highlights the location of a block in the body's energy system. That "block" may be a reflection of a recent stressful period or perhaps some unhealed trauma in the distant past. On occasion, clients experience degrees of pain. I do not cause their pain; it comes, I believe, from the inward flow of energy meeting blockages in their systems. When clients identify pain, I ask that they assign a number to the pain denoting the intensity between one and ten; one represents a mere sensation, and ten represents acute and extreme pain. This identification enables my clients and me to measure their responses as I work and to focus attention on the process rather than on the pain. Paradoxically, pain is not a contraindication during my work. Instead, it should be welcomed as a measurable sign of the healing process. As I continue to manipulate a client's toe or ankle, an energy force created by my connection and movements clears the blockage and eases the pain. Clients will begin to experience the effects of increased energy, such as tingling, waves of energy, or pins and needles at the points where the energy flow had previously been congested by stress or trauma.

What causes these negative congestions in our bodies? As soon as we perceive a frightening stimulus, our body goes into what is termed a "flight or fright" response. Walter Bradford Cannon coined this term in 1915 to describe physiological changes in the body in response to pain, hunger, fear, and rage. This response originates in the ancient part of our mammalian brains, directly connected to our autonomic nervous systems. Our ancestors' lives depended on this autonomic system to outrun or fight various creatures, such as saber-toothed tigers. Each wanted the other for dinner.

This autonomic response causes our bodies to flood with adrenocorticotropic hormones, otherwise known as stress hormones. Within eight seconds of perceiving a frightening stimulus, each cell in our body floods with these hormones. Conscious action is not required. We are hardwired, so to speak, and each bodily system automatically prepares for the perceived danger. Nowadays, however, that modern saber-toothed tiger may be trouble with our bosses, conflicts in our relationships, and road rage on the freeway.

If we take this understanding a little further, it is easy to hypothesize that every thought we have, both positive and negative, must affect our bodies. Indeed, as soon as a client has a thought, even before he voices it, I can feel a response to that thought in his foot. I recall the first time I became aware of this. I was in Belfast in 1999, treating Jen. She was one of the few people who came to see me for preventative treatments. During one particular session, I felt a sudden and barely perceptible tension in her toe. Assuming she was sensing something, I inquired only to be told no. Instinctively and impulsively, I followed this with, "Well, are you thinking of something?" This time she appeared startled, her face colored, and she looked decidedly uncomfortable. She had indeed been thinking of something, and she assumed that I had read her thoughts. I reassured her that I had not. I advised her that I had simply connected the imperceptible movement in her foot to some "action" on her part. That action turned out to be her thought. For the first time, I realized that every subtle action in a client's foot is a bodily response to something—even the client's very thoughts. This deepened my developing awareness of the enormous power that negative thinking may have in creating many of our illnesses.

The other common occurrence during treatments is a peculiar gurgling sound emanating from the region of the torso. I record this as [FB]—the body's feedback—in my session notes. Again, with experience, I have come to realize that this sound is a signal that a release or healing has occurred. Many clients initially attribute this sound to hunger pangs and resist my more positive explanation. A book by the late Betty Shine, *Mind to Mind*, supports my hypothesis that this sound reflects the clearing and opening up of the body's energy systems.

Advances in physics are now teaching us that the body's cells memorize every traumatic event and that memory is not isolated to the brain cells. This being the case, healing must reach the cellular level to be lasting. During work, clients sometimes describe a "shivery" feeling in the body. In the early days of my work, when clients experienced this and said that they were "cold," I would heap on blankets to no avail. It was not until one client advised me that she had shivered all evening after returning home that I realized something more profound was occurring. It was not the external environment that made clients shiver; it was their internal environments. I now call this "cell healing."

Often, depressed or stressed clients who live excessively in their heads will describe the experience of feeling their brain cells respond as if their cells are readjusting. I believe that the synaptic networks or hardwiring in the brain are being transformed during this process. Thus, habitual negative thinking patterns can be transformed in an instant. On occasion, I have witnessed dramatic changes in how a client views her internal and external worlds.

Let me walk you through a standard session I may have with a client. Imagine a female we will call Susan. Susan has made an appointment ostensibly because she has been diagnosed with a slipped disc. She, as many do, comes to see me as a last resort. She wishes to avoid surgery, but the pain has kept her from her teaching post for two months, and she fears the repercussions of remaining off work. I spend the first hour of our initial two-hour session taking a very detailed history to establish the cause of the physical manifestation. I discover that Susan is a committed teacher and loves teaching, but that she works in an unsupported and deeply stressful environment. Before I attempt to help relieve her spinal problem, it is crucial for her long-term health that we fully explore the root of the problem on an emotional level. Occasionally, a first session does not achieve this, but for full and lasting healing, exploring the emotional roots of physical problems is essential.

Following my detailed questioning and subsequent discussion, Susan is clearer regarding what she will identify as her need during the next stage of our work together. Susan initially said that she wanted "relief from the disc pain." With fresh and deeper insight, she now asks "to receive peace." There is a powerful difference in these statements. I must peel many of the "onion layers" to reach the core of a client's healing need.

Now picture Susan lying almost prone on a couch, feet bare, with her legs slightly elevated. I cover her with a blanket—not for heat, but for comfort. I recognize how vulnerable she feels at this point. No amount of telling people how safe they are will sink in at this stage. They need to experience the safety of our journey together, which they do. I advise Susan to keep her eyes closed throughout the entire process. This enables her to keep her focus on the here and now, minimizing external distractions, and allows her to be more sensitive to what occurs internally. This is essential if I am to support her to a level of higher consciousness.

I start by gently stretching the right foot, so gently and slowly that it is barely perceptible. Susan, as with the majority of clients, has a gradual sense of her leg becoming longer, and she may feel that I am physically elongating her body. I am not. What I believe may be occurring is that Susan is physically sensing a connection with her myelin sheath, which protects her entire nervous system. Another hypothesis is that she is tuning into cosmic energy. Both may indeed be simultaneously occurring.

Clients regularly report feeling this stretch at various points throughout the body. As much as I recognize that something more powerful is occurring, to be honest, this physiological response remains a mystery to me. At this preliminary stage, I immediately ask Susan for feedback regarding where she feels the stretch in her body. Initially, Susan may experience the stretch simply at the ankle or around the knee. As she allows her body to relax more deeply into the process, this feeling can extend right up to the crown of her head. This is what I am aiming for, as the entire system is then clearly open and free. When Susan advises me that she feels the stretch at the crown, I ask the seemingly absurd question, "Do you get a sense that your crown area is open or closed?" Susan will respond with an emphatic "open," indicating an expanded awareness, or "closed." There is no right or wrong response. The response seems to denote her level of awareness. Susan, as happens with some clients, immediately starts undergoing experiences on a visual level; she may see vivid colors.

Until Susan is comfortable with me and feels safe with this process, this initial stretching may merely be experienced as a pleasant feeling in which her leg seemingly gets longer; then, when I release the pressure, her leg "shrinks" back to the original position. Following the opening exercise, I manipulate her feet. I have no theoretical framework to explain my steps beyond the fact that this relaxes Susan and facilitates an enhanced connection to her physical and higher consciousness. These subtle and gentle movements are a result of higher guidance. Susan, when relaxed, begins shifting to a deeper connection with her energy body and reaches a heightened awareness that extends beyond her physical body, as happens with many clients. As I work, Susan feels various sensations at the points in her body where she has energy blockages. Exceptions, and there are few, exist when a client is so tense or depressed as to be out of touch with his body; in that case, he would not sense anything. In Susan's case, she starts to feel sharp pain in the precise area of her discomfort. The pain noted as a "nine" gradually reduces until it ceases.

Initially in my practice, I learned to watch the eyelids very closely throughout this process for what I then recorded as REM (rapid eye movement), which Kleitman and Aserinsky identified and defined in the early 1950s. Kleitman and Aserinsky ascertained that people in REM dream states are physically paralyzed, incapable of independent movement. However, my clients inexplicably can move their limbs at will while describing what they are visually experiencing. When I observe REM during my treatments, it often, though not always, signifies that the client is seeing something from a higher level of consciousness. In the early days, clients would tell me they had fallen asleep when this occurred. Now that I am alert to this altered state, I talk my clients through this process. More recently, I have noted that REM need not be present for a vision to be occurring. I can only surmise that REM served to alert me initially to the visions, before I had refined my process. Now that I am aware, my higher teachers, whoever they may be, no longer need to prompt me. I make no apologies for an absence of theoretically convenient explanations. During this process, I am consciously out of the driver's seat.

The common manifestations that Susan and 99 percent of my other clients experience may include some or all of the following: tingling or numbness, feeling parts of the body disappearing or elevating, heaviness, moderate discomfort or pain as the energy blockages are cleared, and, on occasion, out-of-body experiences.

This may seem somewhat unnerving to you, and I must admit that it was strange to me initially, too. My clients who are in an elevated state of consciousness report it as nothing unusual. When one client, a middle-aged carpenter I treated a few years ago for a back problem, "left his body" during a session, I was indeed very surprised. I would have expected that experience from someone who was interested in "new age" material or meditated regularly, but neither of these was true of this man. I questioned him later and asked him how he accepted this occurrence so casually. His reply was, "Oh, when the teacher in school used to beat me mercilessly with a stick, I used to leave my body to escape the pain." He was just doing what had come naturally as a child, albeit under very different circumstances.

Ultimately, Susan and many clients experience communication with beings at a higher level of consciousness. All of those I have been honored to work with in India naturally relax into a state in which they achieve deep communication with a higher power or consciousness.

Susan, as with all of my clients, is free to connect with her higher consciousness and with ascended beings—from deceased relatives, to God, Jesus, and angels—during her session. The decision is hers, not mine. A minority of my clients have even contacted and communicated with the higher consciousnesses of other living people. When I ask a client, "What does Jesus or God look like?" they often cannot definitively reply. I now realize that God appears in a form that is "conventional" to each individual, be it in the form of Jesus, Krishna, Buddha, Lakshmi, Allah, or simply the color purple. One man in Mexico, an atheist, had a rewarding conversation with and received wisdom from orbs, reputed to be energy beings. Whatever the visual expression of a higher power, a radiant bright white light is often in the description somewhere.

Admittedly, some of my clients, a small minority, have said that they desired to receive a vision or "meeting" and were disappointed. Included in this group are two of my closest friends. Although having them get their wish would have been so wonderful, I have no explanation when it does not happen. I am only left to speculate that my close relationship with some clients creates an unfortunate barrier, preventing them from fully letting go.

Susan achieves peace, her desired outcome. This is a positive first step for her. Armed with greater awareness regarding the issues surrounding her disability, she can make healthy choices toward wholeness. Many clients will choose at this point to commit to two further meetings to reinforce their long-term healing. One session can have powerful outcomes and be sufficient. I leave the next steps totally up to the client.

THREE: THE MIND-BODY CONNECTION

The truth about our childhood is stored up in our body, and though we can repress it, we can never alter it. Our intellect can be deceived, our feelings manipulated, our perceptions confused, and our body tricked with medication. But someday the body will present its bill, for it is as incorruptible as a child who, while still whole in spirit, will accept no compromises or excuses, and it will not stop tormenting us until we stop evading the truth.

Alice Millar, 1923–2010

Most ancient cultures never questioned the interrelationship between their inner and outer worlds. They intuitively knew that they were connected to all life. They understood that disease was a malady of the spirit, as well as a malady of the body. But somewhere along the way, the delicate marriage of mind-body-spirit became fragmented. Hard science took over, and our mystical connections to nature, God, and ourselves were lost. The more driven by science and sophisticated the medical community became, the wider the chasm grew. Physicians treated the body as if it were a car—nothing more than a collection of parts that required service and repair. Thankfully, the recent integration of science and spirit is fundamentally changing our narrow, separatist view of health and wellness. Mainstream medicine is starting to embrace the idea that stress can and does cause illness and disease and that the mind and body work in synchronicity.

During the 1990s, scientists working with the U.S. Army investigated whether or not the power of our feelings continues to have an effect on living cells, specifically DNA, once those cells are no longer part of the body. In other words, when tissue samples are taken, does emotion still impact extracted cells either positively or negatively? In groundbreaking research, which is detailed more fully by Gregg Braden in *The Divine Matrix*, Dr. Cleve Backster, a U.S. Army scientist and researcher in primary perception, conducted tests that demonstrated the power that emotion has on our cellular structure. His research has demonstrated how our thoughts can actually alter the shape of our basic DNA. The journal *Advances* reported a study in 1993 that DNA swabs taken from a donor could be measured electrically and shown to respond emotionally to the person they came from. Science demonstrates more and more support for what people have previously regarded as mystical nonsense.

The old paradigms and their limiting beliefs are crumbling, and alternative paradigms—including ones much more ancient than mainstream science—are coming in out of the cold. These approaches, such as the ancient medical practices of ayurveda and acupuncture, recognize the body as a microcosm coexisting with the greater biosphere. Dr. Samuel Hahnemann, a German physician, discovered homeopathy nearly two hundred years ago. Homeopathy uses active ingredients in minute dosages along with naturally occurring substances in order to provide a healthier balance in our internal chemistry. In mainstream medicine, these minute dosages are generally viewed as ineffective. Visit a homeopath and she is as likely to ask the question, "Do you like sweet or sour foods?" as she is to ask, "Where is the pain?" We are traveling full circle, returning to the more holistic view of the human being that was held by Hippocrates and other forefathers of medicine.

In chapter two, I mentioned that stress kicks the body into "fight or flight" mode in eight seconds, flooding every cell with adrenocorticotropic hormones (ACTH). Every organ in the body is affected. A certain amount of stress is essential for our daily existence. Without it, we could not even stand erect or carry out the simplest of mundane tasks. This natural stress response from our mammalian autonomic system does us no harm. Our body holds amazing powers of rejuvenation and will quickly regain homeostasis following the occasional stress overload, stemming from exams, moving home, etc. What I refer to as "sustained negative stress," however, can and will eventually cause a breakdown of the immune system, leaving it prone to disease. Our body is engineered to release stress hormones through activity. In recent years, however, we have adopted a more sedentary lifestyle, and obesity rages in many countries. From childhood, we are building the blocks of ill health.

What is not so well documented or understood is the relationship between stress, emotion, and individual parts of the body. Despite the pioneering efforts of many people, mainstream science and medicine have been slow to recognize this phenomenon. Louise Hay, whose groundbreaking book, *Heal Your Life,* identified the particular thought patterns and feelings that correlated to specific body parts, could not get publishers to take her work seriously, and eventually she self-published. Hay House, the publishing company she founded to print her book, is now a worldwide and highly acclaimed company, so clearly the general public is ready to hear her message. Her courageous struggle to be heard has paid off, as now science has caught up and vindicated her teachings.

Far too many of us hide our feelings, stuff our emotions, and bury our deepest fears and sorrows, thinking we are putting our pain behind us. Men are especially vulnerable to this. Medical research shows that men have an increased risk of heart attack within six months of experiencing a significant loss in a relationship or career. Our modern, fast moving world has no time or patience for mourning or loss. For all of our sophistication and knowledge, we have no idea how to deal with deep sorrow and pain. Time and time again, I have discovered that we cannot deny a broken heart without suffering the consequences. Grief needs an outlet; grief needs tears.

The chemical content of tears differs from the watery eyes one gets from smoke, allergies, or dust. Actually, there are three types of tears, all of which have differing chemical makeup: basal, reflux, and emotional. Basal tears keep the cornea clear from dust and protect it against infection. They are most likely directed by out autonomic nervous systems. Reflux tears are those nuisance tears we get when peeling an onion or when an irritant has entered the eye. Our immune systems come into play here. Emotional tears, however, have a different chemical makeup than those for lubrication; emotional tears contain more of the protein-based hormones prolactin, adrenocorticotropic hormone, and leucine enkephalin (a natural painkiller) than basal or reflex tears do. It appears that emotional tears release stress hormones. If tears don't flow out, they flow in—and where the buried feelings go is where these feelings create problems. Groundbreaking work by doctors, such as Dr. Bernie Segal, Patch Adams, and scientists are expanding the vocabulary of medicine to include terms that describe the mind-body oneness in relation to illness.

Many specialist doctors now talk about a "cancer personality," reflecting the ancient philosophy of Hippocrates, the father of medicine, who is credited with the Hippocratic oath that physicians still take today. In the fifth century BC, Hippocrates maintained that it was far more important to know what person the disease has than what disease the person has. According to some of the data available, the cancer personality can be summed up in the following traits: unresolved loss or trauma in childhood, an overwhelming need to please others, feelings of unworthiness, extreme avoidance of conflict, tension in one's parental relationship, and, the trait I believe to be most damaging of all, the harboring of unexpressed anger or resentment.

In October 1981, Ryke Geerd Hamer, a German doctor and cancer surgeon, presented the results of his research with twenty thousand patients at Germany's Tübingen University. According to Pat Thomas, contributing editor of *What Doctors Don't Tell You*, who discussed Dr. Hamer's research in the British newsletter's January 2003 issue,

> X-rays taken of the brain [of cancer patients] by Dr. Hamer have shown a dark shadow somewhere in the brain. These dark spots are located in exactly the same place in the brain for the same type of cancer. There was also a 100 percent correlation between the dark spot in the brain, the location of the cancer in the body, and the specific type of unresolved conflict.
>
> These findings have lead [*sic*] Dr. Hamer to suggest that when we are in a stressful conflict that is not resolved, the emotional reflex center in the brain that corresponds to the experienced emotion (for example, anger, frustration or grief) will slowly break down. Each of these emotion centers is connected to a specific organ. When a center breaks down it will start sending the wrong information to the organ it controls, resulting in the formation of deformed cells in the tissues—in other words, cancer cells.[1]

---

1 Quoted in Cynthia Chatfield, "Ryke Geerd Hamer, MD: The New Medicine," *Healing Cancer,* http://healingcancer.info/ebook/ryke-geerd-hamer (accessed September 21, 2010).

Louise Hay's brave stance is now being vindicated by a much slower science. I worked with a woman who had been physically abused by her mother. On one occasion, when she was around nine years of age and standing with her back to her mother, she suddenly felt the lash of a leather whip across her forehead. The tail of the whip cut into her upper face at the side of her eye. The physical wound healed quickly. The emotional wound went much deeper. Forty years later, she developed a basal cell carcinoma—skin cancer—at precisely the spot where she had been injured. Coincidence? I think not. Yet another female client visited me following a diagnosis of early arthritis. I discovered that she was experiencing a lot of conflict in her job. Once she resolved her own inner conflict, her "arthritis" disappeared.

Thanks to quantum mechanics, the entanglement theory, numerous studies, and the rising voices of so many visionaries, alternative and holistic therapies are no longer dismissed as quackery or delusion.

The following experiences of Joseph and Pat illustrate how suppressed emotions manifest and express themselves unconsciously in the body.

Joseph

I met Joseph toward the end of 2001, while spending the first of two winters in southern Spain. We were both helpers at a dog sanctuary outside Nerja. When I offered to volunteer my services at the dog sanctuary, I was asked how I wanted to help. "Give me a task that you need done. I am here to help," I rashly said. Hanna, the owner, promptly gave me the unpleasant task, which other volunteers avoided, of cleaning excrement from the kennels. This was where I met Joseph. A chef by profession, Joseph appeared to be around forty years old, with the most soulful eyes I have yet to meet in a man. He hailed from Scotland and had moved to Spain with his partner the previous summer to work as the senior chef in a local hotel. Like me, he loved dogs, but circumstances prevented him from having one of his own. Now and then, he would relieve me by taking a few of the more excitable dogs out for a walk while I cleaned up their messes. At tea break one day, we shared our stories. Joseph told me that although otherwise physically fit, he was having difficulty carrying out his chef duties because of a sudden cramping in his left hand's third finger. It would lock in a bent position for no apparent reason and had already caused a few accidents in the kitchen. Despite numerous visits to his doctor, no clinical explanation was found. When he asked me for advice, I offered him a treatment.

The following week, Joseph came to my apartment, and I took a brief history. He was a widower. His wife had died two years previously from cancer. For four years, Joseph had nursed her. He described watching her slowly and painfully die and added that sometimes when he closed his eyes, he could still see her stricken, gaunt face. "She was like a skeleton when she died," he sorrowfully told me. I felt compassion for this gentle man and realized that he was still grieving. I also briefly wondered whether he could commit to his new partner, when he appeared not to have said goodbye to his wife.

Having taken this history, I prepared for Joseph's treatment and explained the process. He relaxed relatively quickly for someone new to my work and immediately reported feeling sensations in various parts of his body. I was surprised that, although he was sensitive to all I was doing, he reported that he felt nothing at all in the problem finger. I was gently manipulating Joseph's foot, when I instinctively asked, "Are you aware of seeing anything, Joseph?"

His reply startled me. "I can see Maura's face." He said this calmly, and his face looked peaceful. "Her face looks healthy; there's no trace of illness. She has such a smiling face." There was a long period of silence, and I studied Joseph's face, looking for signs of distress. "She's happy for me," he said. Joseph shed no tears, and he demonstrated no signs of painful emotion. From his serene expression, I could tell that he was at peace.

We casually reviewed the session during our tea break the following Saturday at the dog shelter. With a beaming smile, Joseph told me that his finger had ceased to be a problem! It was only then that he admitted to having mixed feelings about entering a new relationship with Catherine, his current partner. He had been wracked with guilt about what he perceived to be disloyalty to his dead wife. The problem finger was, look and behold, his ring finger! Joseph's relationship with Catherine ceased that summer. Ironically, it was she who ended it, deciding that she was not ready to make a long-term commitment. Joseph admitted to me that in contrast to his ambiguous feelings regarding the relationship, he had been very clingy with Catherine and realized that he had jumped too quickly into the relationship. He felt that when the time was right, he would be more honestly available to another person.

When we refuse to honor and express our innermost feelings, our bodies express them for us.

Pat's Story

A sixty-four-year-old principal of an accounting firm, Pat had heard about my work through a radio interview and booked an appointment to see me about a chronic bladder problem. When Pat walked into my treatment room, I immediately noticed his inflexible walk and very rigid posture. Although he smiled a greeting, his stiff smile held no warmth. A red and blotchy neck gave away his nervousness, and Pat confirmed his discomfort shortly upon sitting down. I showed him my session record sheet. He sharply replied that he "didn't share personal details with other people." I outlined why I needed the information and discussed the process involved in my initial briefing. I reiterated the boundaries of confidentiality and stressed how important his history was, as its essence held the triggers for his current illness. Pat gave me a swift, scathing, and skeptical look, a look that I recognized only too well. He agreed to share his story. My fleeting thought was that it takes a skeptic to know a skeptic.

Pat had been diagnosed with neurogenic bladder disease three years previously. Unfortunately, this disease resulted in chronic urinary retention, which is a condition that keeps the bladder from ever fully emptying, culminating in recurring urinary tract infections. Despite visits to a top UK consultant, he was given no prospect of a cure. He was given long-term prescriptions of antibiotics and was forced to use catheterization to ensure he fully emptied his bladder and to prevent the potentially damaging infections. All of this was personally distressing for Pat, particularly in social settings, and it was having dramatic effects on his professional and personal life. He was adept at managing the problem on a physical level, meticulously avoiding any serious infections, but he found the emotional impact extremely distressing. Pat was accustomed to being in control of his life. Now the tables were turned, and he was at the mercy of a catheter and urine bag. Every measure of liquid had to be evaluated. A casual pint at his local bar took on a whole new significance. "Any spontaneity in my life is gone," he told me.

During the history, Pat told me that he had separated from his wife after twenty-seven years of what he described as an unhappy and unfulfilled marriage. He maintained that he had never really loved her and had stayed in the marriage for the sake of the children. Following further probing, however, he grudgingly revealed that his wife had actually left him for another man. Pat admitted that he was truly "pissed off" by the fact that he had struggled with increasing unhappiness for so many years, only to have his wife leave him in the end.

On two occasions during this initial session, Pat bitterly remarked, "I held back continuously." This Freudian repetition alerted me to the possibly unconscious trigger for his urinary problems. When he told me that his bladder problem was diagnosed shortly after the separation, I confirmed the connection. I asked Pat if he had felt "totally pissed off" during this period. He affirmed that he did, adding that this was most definitely an understatement of how he truly felt. He also admitted to feeling "very bitter toward my wife." He said this with a tightly clenched jaw, while simultaneously making a fist with both hands. I questioned him about this. "Yes, I do grind my teeth at night. How did you know?" I said that it was my job to notice signs and signals. If fact, had I not noticed his tightly clenched jaw, his severely worn bottom teeth were a sure give away. His resentment and anger were palpable, and I wondered how open he would he be to healing. Beyond the angry exterior, however, I could sense a tired and broken spirit.

Upon further questioning, I sensed that Pat was pissed off about many other things in his life. A clear pattern was emerging. Pat continually did things for others to the extent that he ended up feeling unappreciated and subsequently resentful. His life story was that of giving thankless service to others without any reciprocation. I had an image of him being consumed with long held bitterness, and I hesitated to confront him. This presented me with a dilemma. If I confronted Pat with what I suspected was his martyrdom, his "after all I have done for them" attitude, I suspected that he might walk out. However, if I neglected to tell him what I suspected, I would be ultimately of no help to his potential healing. In fact, not to confront him would have made me complicit in his unhealthy pathology.

I have learned from years of experience that physical healing is often temporary if the underlying cause is not therapeutically addressed. Sometimes I need to work like a sleuth in my attempts to uncover the root cause of a particular presenting disease, which frequently has its root in early childhood. I chose to take the risk with Pat and proceeded to draw a circle on a blank sheet of paper. On it I replicated the "Cycle of Suffering," included here in figure 1.

CYCLE OF SUFFERING

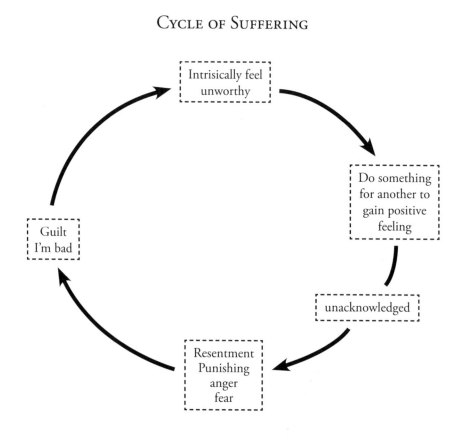

Figure 1 The Cycle of Suffering

I explained that many of us feel intrinsically unworthy. Some of us perform an act of kindness for others or a significant other in order to feel good about ourselves. We do not explain that we have an ulterior, and many times unconscious, motive for this act. The unconscious thought process is, "If I do this act of kindness for you, you will appreciate me, and then I will be able to feel conditionally good about myself. If you like me, then I can like myself." This is such a powerful and seductive trap.

In my career, I challenged many of my social work students to recognize and release this pre-burnout martyrdom malady. I further explained to Pat that because those we perform our good deeds for are unaware of our often unconscious and unexpressed contracts, they do not provide the necessary appreciation or "drip feed" necessary for our feelings of self-worth. Our action, designed to receive love, is often then made futile and unacknowledged. Our feelings, if not immediately, will eventually turn to negativity, resentment, and anger, which in turn will make us feel guilty. Before we know it, we feel even more unworthy. The cycle continues ad infinitum. Doesn't it just sound impossible? It is impossible for our self-worth to receive such constant reinforcement from outside. Just as the hamster is destined to a cyclical life on the wheel, we forever travel round and round in circles seeking external affirmation and love. It is a futile and fraught journey.

In clinical terms, this condition is referred to as "object referral." In object referral, we constantly need the approval of others. When I first started my training post within the social services in 1990, I was teaching perhaps twenty-one participants in a program. Despite glowing feedback from twenty of the participants, I would focus on the one anonymous participant who did not appreciate my teaching. I would allow the one to consume my attention, wondering where I went wrong. In object referral, we also feel an intense need to control things, power, and people. Our needs are based on fear. Objects, people, circumstances, and experiences outside ourselves influence us. In contrast to the servitude of object referral, in "self-referral" our internal reference points are our own spirits, not the objects of our experience. The Louise Hay philosophy shows us that the thoughts we choose to think are the tools we use to create our lives. Breaking this self-destructive pattern of behavior is not easy, but it is preferable to spending a lifetime on the endlessly spinning wheel, unconsciously allowing our negativity to manifest in serious illness, as it did with Pat for many unrewarding years.

When Pat actually nodded in recognition as he listened to my explanation, I was relieved and pleasantly surprised. It was, in fact, a relief for him to see his pattern of behavior in a safe, non-judgmental way. I was pleased that he had not walked out at this early stage of our work together. My explanation fit like a glove for him—an uncomfortably familiar glove. This was not a new pseudo psychology. For the first time, Pat admitted that he could see his dysfunctional and erroneous behavior with love and a great deal of compassion.

Despite initial resistance, the majority of people who are exposed to this Cycle of Suffering will acknowledge and ironically welcome its somewhat blunt view of their unhealthy behavior. When we see the pattern, we have choices available to us. Being on the wheel is exhausting, because, as you can imagine, you ultimately never really get anywhere! Well you do, actually; you get to a spinning place of endless suffering.

During our hands-on session, Pat took a long time to relax—but considering the sensitive and challenging work we had done beforehand, this was not surprising. In fact, his feet were so stiff and unyielding that I thought he would experience little. Then he jumped, and his whole body went stiff. I immediately asked, "Are you feeling something uncomfortable, Pat?" He did not reply. Although I had advised him that because his presenting problem was in the genital region, he would most likely experience sensations there, he obviously had not anticipated what I now expected he was sensing. I continued, "Are you okay with this, Pat?"

"Yes," he managed to whisper. Despite answering in the affirmative, his body resistance and tone suggested he was not in the least bit comfortable.

"Do you want me to stop Pat? You are completely in charge."

"I'm okay, but it is becoming painful."

Judging by his pained expression, I suspected the pain was acute. "On a scale of one to ten, Pat, if one was just a sensation and ten was extremely painful, what number would you give the pain?"

"Eleven," he replied through clenched teeth. His words were in fact superfluous, as the extent of his discomfort was visible in his contorted expression.

"That's good, Pat, something is shifting, clearing. Are you willing to stay with it? Remember, you are totally in charge."

"Yes."

I was pleased that the area concerned was being triggered. We worked for the rest of the hour, with Pat experiencing sensations in his body where he had old sporting injuries. The session ended without any further sensations in the genital region.

Pat cancelled his next session on the pretext of work. I did not hear from him for a number of weeks. I was disappointed, but not surprised. A small number of clients will take the first step, and despite the session being positive and eventful, for whatever reason they will not continue on the path to healing with me.

Two months later, Pat called me. He was in the hospital with another infection, a serious one. Sounding very depressed and fearful, he asked if I would visit. A few days later, I did. Pat admitted that the period following our first session had been very challenging. He confessed, "I have been brought to my knees, and I now realize that I am the cause of my own misery." He said it had taken this most recent infection for him to acknowledge the correlation between his rancid thoughts and feelings and his bodily response.

I do not want to suggest here that all people with similar diseases to Pat's will have had the same root cause. No two people are the same. I simply wish to use his experience as an illustration of the mind-body oneness. However, I firmly believe that everything that manifests in the body has its roots in thought and emotion. Surgeons can successfully excise the cancerous tumor, but if we do not excise the accompanying root of negative thoughts and feelings, we run the risk of reoccurrence years later. Readers who want to explore this subject further may wish to refer to the extensive work of Louise M. Hay on the subject.

I worked with Pat over a number of months. I suspected that changing his pattern of behavior and his long-term view of the world was a challenge for him. He experienced happenings in his world that on the surface appeared to feed into his "after all I did for them" pattern and confirm his negativity. Any healing that Pat derived from our sessions alleviated his symptoms for only a few weeks. Deep down, I knew that Pat had too much invested in his belief system, and, at sixty-four years old, Pat would find change to be almost as traumatic as maintaining his status quo. I freely admit that receiving treatments with me did not remove his problem. They couldn't. I work in close partnership with those I treat. Pat's problem stemmed from deeply rooted thoughts and beliefs, and, sadly, his self-fulfilling prophecy never let him down. The path to potential health was, for him, just as daunting as his illness.

My Personal Anecdote

For many years, I was immobilized by irregular bouts of acute lower back pain. Sometimes it took merely turning in the bed to trigger a painful assault that lasted for days. It took an astute and intuitive cranial osteopath to alert me to the fact that as soon as I was facing any change in my life, my body negatively responded through unconscious fear. Paradoxically, as soon as I received a promotion in work, a change I regarded on a conscious level as positive, I would be crippled within days! In fact, gaining a promotion was the worst culprit. As soon as my cranial osteopath helped me make the connection, however, the problem ceased.

As I approached any major changes in my life, I made sure to have back-up help, in the form of additional therapeutic massage appointments, arranged well in advance. This coping mechanism, combined with gradually letting go of my fear of change, has resulted today in a nearly perfect back. Nowadays when I get the odd twinge, I book a massage posthaste. It has become my welcome early warning signal.

Reflections

What is your recurring problem? Is it a pain in the neck, feeling stabbed in the back, difficulty digesting things, or tension headaches? Where is the weak link in your physical chain? Whatever recurring problem you have, examine it a little closer. Could it possibly have a correlation with some pattern of stress in your life? Spend a few minutes asking that painful part of you what message it may be attempting to impart. You could be surprised at the answer you receive. By tuning in and listening to your body, you could save a lot on medical bills … not to mention having a happier and more peaceful life! It all starts and ends with a thought. Make your thoughts be of health and joy.

Natural forces within us are the true healers of disease.
Hippocrates, the Father of Medicine

FOUR: LIFE AFTER DEATH

This mortal life is but an intricate journey with many twists and turns, with darkness and light. We journey from the eternal source of all, love, and in the correct time, we return to love.

Katherine Connon, Skeptical Healer

I know with absolute certainty that there is life after death. What that actually means remains a mystery to me. A friend questioned me as she helped shape this book, "Aren't you curious? I can't believe that you don't talk to your clients about their afterlife experiences and the deceased people they communicate with during your sessions." As strange as it may seem, I am not curious. People who report having "near death experiences" describe strikingly similar occurrences from the time they were pronounced clinically dead. I have personally met with and listened to the experiences of two such people. I do not doubt the veracity of their experiences or that they encountered something inexplicable. Was it heaven, as many believe it to be, or a return to our ultimately formless consciousness? Does what we believe make a difference in what we see? I do not know and am honestly not really interested in having an answer at this moment in my life. I feel that we are meant to live a body-mind-spirit life as authentically as we can here on earth, with whatever challenges that brings.

That philosophy may seem to conflict with the work that I do. I do not think so. The particular gift I have been blessed with is to help clients raise their consciousnesses while here on earth and connect to a loving, living, and joyful God in the present.

I am satisfied that a state of humanly incomprehensible unconditional love awaits us when we leave our bodies and return to spirit. I am aware that I came from the source of all to experience mortal life in this body—to experience precisely what I am experiencing. The more years I live, the more I trust in a pure and loving entity giving me precisely what I need. I am content to wait and see. All will unfold in its correct time.

The following four accounts demonstrate the continuance of spirit after death. Two of the stories stem from my personal experience, and two are accounts of grieving parents who reconnected in spirit with their deceased children, finding solace and peace.

My Story

Spiritually reconnecting with my late father satisfied any lingering doubts I may have had regarding the continuance of the soul. His death in 1991 stimulated a remarkable change in my spiritual and emotional life. My feelings regarding God and spirit had been pretty ambiguous following the death of Mammy twenty-four years earlier.

One of the first irrational thoughts that came to me upon hearing of my father's sudden death from a heart attack was, *this will be the last time that I will need to feel this depth of pain.* Although it was a rite of passage I knew I needed to go through, I had anticipated that his death would devastate me. During the last years of his life, I spent a great deal more time with him. Despite our regular and sometimes heated differences of opinion, we had become close. Sundays and Thursdays were my regular times with him. I was his "jack of all trades," carpenter, barber, manicurist, pot repairer, and personal shopper, all rolled into one. I was his general "fixer." I would bake twenty-four small cakes each week, which he would meticulously pack into a number of bags for his freezer. Each day, he would remove a bag and treat himself and, occasionally, his faithful driver. Before I left his home each week, I would thread two needles, one with black thread and one with white. With his pre-threaded needles, he would crudely sew together the holes he regularly burned in his clothes from smoking his pipe. His sewing skills left a lot to be desired, and his clothes resembled garments that would have been more at home on a scarecrow, but it gave him something to do. He certainly was not vain or clothes conscious.

I expected to miss these things about him and all the other rituals, all of my fixing of things in his house. Despite fighting regularly with my father, I loved him. In the depths of my being, I also knew that he loved me, as he did equally all his children; but, like so many Irish parents of his generation, he could not show it in hugs or words. In fact, the only time I remember him expressing feelings toward me was only a number of months prior his death. Ironically, it came during one of our angriest exchanges ever. His words, "You know I care for you," though not uttered in the most loving of contexts, caused me to stop in mid-sentence. I was stunned that my father would express any feelings, least of all anything positive, for the one child he fought with the most. It took time and maturity for me to become aware and accept that the attributes that antagonized me about my father were the same ones I can now accept and acknowledge in myself.

Daddy was always bailing me out financially. If there was a crooked used car salesperson around, I found him and made a purchase. I had an unerring ability to attract con artists and scoundrels. If only my innate skepticism had been transferable to finances, I could have saved thousands of dollars. My various cars were continually breaking down, and I regularly borrowed from my dad to pay for repairs. On one occasion, he sustained a back injury push-starting my stubborn car, a car that would have been more at home between the jaws of a crusher in a car dismantler's yard. I felt guilty about that for years, especially when it would flare up and bother him.

Following his sudden death from a heart attack, I did not grieve as deeply for my father as I had feared I would. Instead of missing him terribly, from the day of his funeral I suddenly and inexplicably felt much closer to him, with a greater depth of loving intimacy between us than when he was alive. The connection felt incredibly strong.

I had many dreams after his death in which he seemed to be giving me messages. Though I could not make any real sense of what they meant, they still brought comfort. Two months after his death, I enrolled in a dream workshop run by a Father Paddy Howell, a gentle, gifted priest from Athenry in County Galway, to enable me to understand what was going on in my dreams. Guided to record each dream and supported in ways to analyze and understand them, I judiciously followed Father Paddy's instructions and even bought a tape recorder to simplify the frequently drowsy early morning recording process. One morning, I awoke from a dream in which my father yet again starred. In the dream, he was driving a car, an action he had not done in years after having had a serious road accident. I was walking along a familiar road near the family home, and he pulled up alongside me. Even in the dreaming state, I recall being surprised that he was behind the wheel of a car. He said, "I cannot be with you and cannot look after your cars any more. Please move your car to the side of the house."

I vaguely remember asking him, "Why?"

He just insisted, "Move your car to the side of the house, Kate."

I glanced at the clock; it was 4:05 am. The dream seemed senseless, and for once, as I was feeling heavy with sleep, I did not even bother to record it. I must have resumed sleep immediately because at 4:16 am, I again awoke, this time abruptly, to the sound of a loud crash outside my bedroom window. I jumped out of bed and raced to the window, only to find that my precious car had just been demolished by what turned out to be a hit and run driver. In shock, I called the police. They arrived quickly and, although sympathetic, advised me that the people responsible were probably long gone and would be difficult to trace.

Once I had provided details for their police statistics, I returned to bed feeling despondent. I did not consider the dream at the time, feeling too wrapped up in self-pity to consider anything beyond the immediate disastrous loss. Sleep would not come. Something kept nagging at me to return to the car. It was nothing dramatic like a voice, but something imperceptible that I could not identify kept urging me to go down to the car. The nagging persisted no matter how I attempted to ignore it and get some sleep. I knew that the next day would be a stressful one. Maybe I had left something in it, I reasoned; perhaps I should check that it was locked.

Reluctantly, I got up, pulled a dressing gown over my nightclothes, and went down to look at the car. It was then I spotted some liquid at the point of impact, and a few feet away, where the car, I suspected, had turned the corner, were more droplets of liquid. Still in my nightclothes, I walked the block of about ten houses to the next corner, and sure enough, there were further drops of liquid. Carrying on around the next few blocks, I followed the path of the hit-and-run driver. Had I been spotted, I would have looked like a most unusual Sherlock Holmes—head bowed, walking slowly down the road in my dressing gown and slippers at 5 am on a misty, cold winter morning, following the trail of my hit and run driver. About ten minutes into my detective work, the drops finally laid their last clue at the gateway to a semi-detached house. In the driveway, facing inward toward the back of the driveway, a car was parked. From the rear, it looked to be in immaculate condition. I cautiously approached the car, and there it was: the hit-and-run car with its entire front crumpled like a battered old concertina. I wondered briefly how they had managed to drive the car home. The front of the car was now just an angry piece of mangled metal. I ran back home and called the police. They listened, incredulous, to my story, but dutifully went to the address I provided.

The car was undoubtedly the one that had almost demolished mine. The police went to the house, checked out the car, knocked on the door, and a man answered. He said that his wife had driven it, but that she was now in bed sleeping. Going to the bedroom, the police found her with the bedclothes over her head, fully dressed. She was so intoxicated she could not stand, and the police arrested her.

Afterward, with the excitement and adrenaline rush over, the realization of what had happened set in. Thoughts returned to my father, who had bailed me out so often in life and could not let go so quickly in death. He had attempted to forewarn me. On failing that, he "nudged" me to return to the scene. If I had not returned to the car when I did, the droplets, which turned out to be from the smashed radiator, would have dried up by morning. If I had paid attention to the warning from him in the first place, however, would events have turned out differently? Maybe someday, if I am still interested, I will find out! The experience was wonderful. Not only was I able to get a new, albeit secondhand car, but far more importantly, I did not need blind faith to believe in life after death. I had my very own firsthand evidence of the continuance of the spirit. I felt my father's presence for many months after he died, and during a challenging period, the dreams gave me incredible comfort. The father I knew in the flesh had numerous faults, but thankfully, he also had many strengths and positive traits that I admired. My father in spirit was a perfect source of comfort.

Annie's Story

I had one more fleeting experience of life after the death of the body. Annie, an elderly, terminally ill woman I treated for some time from 1995 to 1998, gave me a brief insight. Annie lived in the hinterland of a Protestant/Catholic working-class estate in Belfast, and was highly respected by neighbors, both Catholic and Protestant. The respect Annie's often warring neighbors extended to her went way beyond sectarianism. She was a special lady. She had been terminally ill for so long that her loving family seemed to be caught in a web of anticipatory grief. She had a loving relationship with all of her children. More than her children, however, Annie loved her husband of forty years with a passion. She was a rotund, tough, honorable woman with a heart of gold, and I could easily understand the love and affection her family had for her.

Annie told me that she liked to visit me so that she could have a laugh—and laugh she did. I was fond of Annie, and I laughed a lot with her, as well. Annie talked to me freely about her death and was at peace with herself and her multifaceted illness. I once suggested that if I died first, I would let her know what heaven was like and asked her to do the same for me. She agreed. We had a pact.

The night Annie returned fully to spirit I had a dream about her. In the dream I could see her walking down a broad street. In front of the street was some kind of vague symbolic barrier. The scene was reminiscent of the Gary Cooper walk in the film *High Noon*. As Annie approached the barrier, it just faded, and Annie seemed to float down the street. Maybe the dream that night was my fertile imagination, but on the night Annie died, I like to think that she kept her promise.

That was not the last of Annie, however. One evening, about a year after her death, she was to resurface. When I visit Belfast, I often visit with her daughter Cate, a good friend and fellow Gestalt trainee. On this occasion, I was giving Cate a treatment for a lingering headache. Finally relaxing into the session, she said she felt the headache lifting. Simultaneously, I gradually became aware of a faint smell of roses wafting across my face. Initially, I believed that I was sensing Cate's perfume, but I knew that rose scent was not her style. Then I wondered if it could be Annie. I contemplated the prospect for a few minutes, rationalizing dismissively that that kind of thing does not really happen, and put it down to imagination. But the faint aroma of roses persisted. Like the apostle Thomas, I inwardly bargained for a sign. No sooner had I expressed the silent challenge than Cate squealed, "Ah, something sharp just prodded my back!" I stared at Cate's prone figure on the couch. With her eyes closed, however, she had already resumed her relaxed state. *Annie is here*, I thought with a shock. I froze for a moment. I decided against mentioning this to Cate, worried about how she would react. For the rest of the session, I was unusually silent, aware that Annie had been or perhaps was still in the room with us. When I finished my work, I went to the bathroom to wash my hands and to take some time to decide if I should tell Cate what I had experienced, unsure if my experience would comfort or distress her. Whatever her response, I decided Cate had a right to know.

When I returned to the room where we had worked, I told her exactly what had occurred and what I had felt. Cate was moved and grateful. I sensed, however, that Cate's partner, Peter, who had been sitting in the corner of the room throughout our work together, was not entirely happy at this turn of events. He remained quiet.

Early the following morning, I was giving Peter, a mountain climber, a treatment for a sustained back and ankle injury. The treatment progressed uneventfully. However, after the treatment, something strange happened. His eight-year-old daughter had been coming in and out of the room during the session. When Peter opened his eyes, he startled me by asking his daughter immediately, "Did you spray perfume on me while I was lying here?" She said no. I believe that Annie may have been the cause of the aroma and that she was trying to dispel any lingering doubts Peter may have had regarding her presence the previous night. Peter made no further reference to his experience, but his face took on a thoughtful expression and he briefly shrugged his shoulders.

Many times since then I have, through my clients, realized again and again how those who are no longer with us physically are often closer to us in spirit. As we shift to a higher consciousness, our experiences and understandings of space and time must grow, as well.

As an addendum to Cate's experience, this year I again treated her. During our work together, she met and spoke with Annie. While they met, I asked Cate if Annie had any message for me. Annie simply said through Cate, "Didn't I tell you before? Everything is perfect."

Yes you did, Annie.

Olivia

In the late spring of 2005, I was enjoying my garden on a wonderful balmy and sunny April morning. The town I live in, Westport, County Mayo, is widely acknowledged as the most beautiful town on the west coast of Ireland. As I relaxed in the sun, I received a call from Mary, who runs a bed-and-breakfast business in Westport. Mary was calling to ask if I could treat a person staying at her bed-and-breakfast. When I inquired about the reason, she immediately passed the phone to Olivia, who, with anxiety ringing in her voice, asked to meet me that evening. On hearing the reason for her request, I immediately agreed, and we arranged a mutually convenient time.

When I opened the door to Olivia's knock that evening, I was met with a face so full of pain that it was impossible to see beyond the agony of her grief. When I first took in her collapsed frame and puffy reddened face, I placed her at around sixty. I invited her to my treatment room and made her comfortable while I detailed my work and the process involved. Olivia proceeded to give me the details of her young daughter Nicky's accidental death just five months earlier. Nicky's final words to her mother had been in a cheerful text she sent while traveling home on the school bus. Upon leaving the bus, she was critically injured by a speeding car. Her life support was turned off within a few days.

During the initial interview, Olivia reiterated that she should have returned to work as a teacher by now. I was not surprised by her comment. She, like so many others in our modern society, felt that she should have snapped out of it by now. The late Elisabeth Kübler-Ross, a Swiss-born psychiatrist, worked with the dying and bereaved for most of her career and taught many students in the field, including myself. She continually reminded us of how important it is to honor the grieving process. Her book *On Death and Dying* (1969) remains an essential read for those wishing to explore the subject further. Less sophisticated cultures understand how essential it is to grieve, yet we have been conditioned to keep a stiff upper lip and resume life within a prescribed timescale.

During our session, Olivia chronologically related what she knew of the last hours of Nicky's life. She told me enough about her daughter for me to realize that she had lost a precious and special child on the brink of adulthood—a child loved by her peers, who had been the best friend to her older sister, Alana. Nicky's sudden death had affected many, just as her remarkable short life had done. Despite having the support of her mother and a new partner and good friend, Olivia was devastated by the tragic, sudden loss of her youngest child. This was not the natural order of things. A child is meant to outlive her parents, not be buried by them. I understood her grief.

As I listened to Olivia's recent history, however, I realized that she described not one, but three losses in her life over the previous few years. The death of her husband seven years earlier had been followed by her loss of Nicky's sister, Alana, when Alana left home to enroll in college just months before Nicky's death. One after another, Olivia had lost her family members. Her stark loneliness and pain were palpable.

Olivia disclosed that she was forty-eight years old, not the worn out sixty she appeared, prematurely aged by grief. Like so many recently bereaved people, Olivia was not on the best of terms with God and, in fact, had quite ambivalent feelings toward him. Having faced the same feelings in my early teens, I could sympathize with her.

As we spoke, I noticed that Olivia's breathing was very shallow. She held her hands in front of her mouth, as if to restrain any possible tears. As I questioned her, she acknowledged that breathing was difficult and that it was almost impossible to take a deep breath. She mentioned the yawning she frequently experienced, so common to deeply bereaved people. Her body was literally crying out for release. When I inquired where in her body she most acutely felt the pain of her loss, she outlined for me a litany of complaints: a sharp pain in the left side of her head, resulting in almost daily headaches, discomfort at the base of her skull, deteriorating eyesight, and heaviness in her chest. On an emotional level, she was finding sleep almost impossible, dropping off around 3 am most nights. From her appearance, it was clear that any sleep she was getting did not rejuvenate her. She also reported frequent panic attacks and was under treatment from her general practitioner. She added that while she was getting counseling support, she felt the benefits to be minimal.

When I completed taking Olivia's history, I outlined my work method and process. I also cautioned that a few people see things or persons during a session and asked how she would feel if she did. I always make that statement specifically in that way for two reasons. I do not wish a client to be shocked by a sudden vision, and also, conversely, I do not wish to disappoint someone should he not see anything. Of course, in my heart, I prayed that she would see Nicky. Having made Olivia comfortable in the chair and stressing, as I had earlier in our conversation, that she was in charge, I commenced work. As I gently stretched her right leg, Olivia experienced tingling sensations in the problem areas that she had earlier identified. Then, as I imperceptibly rotated her toe I noticed her eyelids flicker. Thinking she was seeing something, I asked her if she was. Her response was immediate.

"A yellow ring, a half ring."

"Anything else?"

"No."

"Do you see something?" I asked her again after observing REM.

"I thought I saw an angel … I thought I saw Christ!"

"What does he look like, Olivia?"

"He was standing with his arms outstretched toward me … but he's gone."

Before she had an opportunity to judge or deny what she saw, I suggested that she trust what she was seeing. She told me that she had a pain in her throat. I asked if she were to give the pain a number between one and ten, what it would be? She responded that it would be a four. I asked her to notice how the pain responded as I rotated her ankle. The pain level rose to five, and Olivia remarked that she also felt a blockage in her throat. I asked her if she could see what the blockage was, and she replied that she could not. I inquired if she felt that there was anything she could do to get rid of the blockage. She surprised me by replying, "I can blow it out." Her breathing became conscious and forceful for a few minutes, and I suspected that was precisely what she was doing, blowing out her stress.

During the first part of the session, Olivia's head gave imperceptible little shudders as if releasing something. I suspected it was all her built-up anguish and tension. Throughout the rest of the session, her shudders recurred intermittently. At one point, she saw a picture of sunlight on water and commented that sunlight on water was something Nicky had liked. On a few occasions, she remarked that she saw yellow, blue, orange, and green colors. Another time she saw yellow dots through one eye only, a phenomenon I do not yet understand physiologically. As the session progressed, she looked more and more peaceful. At the end of the treatment, I left her for a few minutes to go and wash my hands and to allow her the space to reconnect and ground herself in her own time.

On my return to the room, Olivia remarked quite calmly, "Nicky came. She hugged me the way she used to, and then someone came for her and she left. She didn't look back. It was a hug for me, not for her." She explained that Nicky had often run to her for the comfort of a hug. The hug between them this morning was subtly but poignantly different. Olivia knew that this time, she was the one receiving that comfort.

"She didn't look back. She is okay. She came, and then she was taken away."

"Who came for her?"

"I believe it was Christ. I did not see them."

We discussed this vision a little more. Despite not seeing her daughter through physical eyes, Olivia was using a sense that I cannot fully comprehend or explain. Some of my previous clients would see in this way, but not with corporeal eyes. The only way I can describe this phenomenon is that they are seeing beyond the senses we know; they are seeing spiritually. When I first left the room after our session, though I never mentioned this to Olivia, I had felt disappointment on her behalf that she had not seen her daughter. Someday I will learn to trust fully. This session did not instantaneously heal Olivia's loss. She bore the pain of her bereavement for many months, but the sense of her daughter fully at peace with Christ gave her, as she put it months later when I requested permission to use her experience here, "peace in my pain and a faith in the God I had also nearly lost."

In the following account, one of my clients, Rachel, had a similar experience of spiritually reconnecting with a young son who had died in a farm accident.

Rachel's Story

Following a local radio interview I did in the summer of 2006, I worked with a deeply bereaved parent, Rachel. Her seventeen-year-old son, Christopher, had died in a farm accident while riding a farm tractor. As Rachel told me about the accident's tragic details and the resulting additional severe stress in her life, I was surprised at how composed she appeared. The only clue to her turmoil was the barely perceptible tightness in her lower jaw. She described the final hours of her son's life and how concerned she was for her two remaining children. She epitomized the devoted parent.

"What do you do with your anger, Rachel?"

Rachel placed her hand on her solar plexus area and said, "People who look at me have no idea what I am going through. People think I have gotten over it. I never let them see how I really feel."

As I listened to Rachel, I could believe that. Apart from her slightly distended face and slouched body, I would not have guessed at the tragedy she was hiding. I am usually perceptive about body language, but she could have fooled me. Had she had not been sitting in front of me and talking very openly about the devastation in her life, I would never have guessed the level of her pain.

Many of us take solace in our work following a loss. It was the contrary in Rachel's case; work often added to her stress, as her customers at the clothing shop she owned made insensitive comments about her loss and behavior. When she had not returned to her business within two weeks, one customer remarked to her colleague, "Doesn't she realize that we are her bread and butter?" I thought I had heard it all, but even I was shocked at this disregard for Rachel's loss. How many others have faced this terrible lack of compassion and understanding after the death of a loved one?

I advised Rachel that she would become seriously ill before she was fifty if she did not express her bottled up emotions. As if in confirmation, she outlined the medical tests she had undergone in the last few years, no doubt because of her additional stress at home. Rachel recognized that they were all previews of what might be in store if she did not deal with her pain.

Prior to beginning the healing work, I asked Rachel what she wanted from the treatment and what she wanted to be different after she had left the room. She replied, "Inner peace. Acceptance that I am doing my best and that I cannot be responsible for the actions of others."

As soon as I began applying tension to her right foot, Rachel reported the sensation of her leg growing longer, and then she reported seeing a triangle on her stomach. It was somewhat unusual for a client to see something of that nature so early in a session. Usually clients need to attain a higher level of relaxation and consciousness prior to seeing something. What occurred next was even more surprising, and it highlighted for me how I was still bracketing off and choosing to ignore some of my clients' intense visual experiences as being just too unusual to be true—even for my mellowing skeptical personality.

"Kate, my stomach and chest feel as if they are on a different level from the rest of me."

I noticed REM. "Rachel, are you seeing something?"

"I see a planet, with a ring around it."

"Like Saturn?"

"Yes. I see a spaceship. I hear the words, 'I love you,' but it is not a sound."

"It is telepathic, Rachel. (I now realize it probably was not telepathy, but some as yet unknown communication.) Who is saying it?"

"Christopher."

My heart never fails to be touched at such revelations. Rachel continued to experience various sensations and experiences.

"My knee is twitching," she said. "I feel very relaxed. I see a flash of a bar on my shoulder … two bolts of light are pushing it off into the chair. You'll think I am losing the plot, Kate! I see a fuzzy ball that is turning into a heart … I see a ball of light … two furry balls in front of me … I see a heart in front of my left eye."

"Just notice and trust what you see, Rachel. You can judge it all you wish later." I continued to manipulate her feet.

"I see a perfect hand reaching out. I see another."

Instantly I knew whom the hands belonged to, but on Rachel's behalf I asked, "Whose hands are they?"

"It's Jesus and Christopher ... I see a light in front of me, a bright white light. It's beaming like a spotlight ... The light was shiny, but I was in a bit of a hollow ... temptation to go closer to the light ... lights swirling around in a circle bringing me to the light."

"Like a vortex, Rachel?"

"Yes. I see a heart-like shape speeding. It stops when I think ... I see a whole lot of trees. There are beams of light coming onto my head. My head is becoming hot. There is sand in my stomach."

Rachel was murmuring almost to herself as I struggled to take it all in. I suspected the sand was a metaphor—perhaps for the weight of the loss she was carrying—and perhaps it was the early signal of a more serious disease. "Can you let go of the sand, Rachel?"

"Yes." With that, Rachel seemed to release and relax. Yes, incredibly, just like that.

"I see the top of a waterfall," she continued. "Below is a green, flat garden. I'm sitting on the edge of the garden, looking toward a sand pit, miles and miles of it ... happy on ... something ... with my hands in the waterfall. I am now walking and lying on the grass. There are loads of flowers, shrubs, and birds. It is a beautiful picture."

The images came fast, as they often do, one after the other, without a break. And then Rachel murmured, "Christopher is there with his dog. He's saying 'I love you, Mam.' He's sending me a big hug. He's gone down a bright tunnel. The colors are even brighter, more bright light coming into my head."

"What color is the light, Rachel?"

"Blue ... green ... I see in the distance little peaks ... there is fog coming off them ... I am floating around, really relaxed."

With this last statement, the session came to a natural close. Leaving Rachel to rest for a few minutes, I left the room to wash my hands and to get water for us both. Rachel looked very peaceful when I returned. I was curious about the dog, as this was the first time that something like this had occurred. Rachel told me that Christopher's dog had died just a month before his accident.

A few days later, Rachel called me, and along with her positive feedback, told me of an unusual and unexpected side effect from her session. When she got into her car, she had to readjust her side mirrors and her rearview mirror. She quite literally left my home not only feeling taller, but she was taller.

Reflections

Do you know someone who has experienced the devastating loss of someone dear? Staying with the pain of others can be difficult. What do you say to help the bereaved? What can you do? Our helplessness in the face of something we cannot "make better" often causes us to avoid the grieving person or resort to inane platitudes. You cannot make pain dissolve, but you can do a simple, although challenging task: listen. The most effective healing tools you have are your ears and your heart. When you listen with an open heart, you help create a space for natural healing to take place. Listen, listen, and listen. Allow the bereaved to express her loss, allow her to play the "old records," even though you may have heard the same story countless times already. Most importantly, encourage tears and more tears. As I've mentioned before, the chemical content of grieving tears is unique, and crying these tears helps release the pain and sorrow. There will come a time for the tears and stories to cease, for life to regain a new but different momentum, but if you can just be there while the pain is most acute, the bereaved will get to a place of peace. You can be her lifesaving bridge to healing grace.

Have you lost someone very dear to you? Was it sudden, or did you receive some warning of impending death? Sudden death leaves so many unanswered questions. Was it painful? What were the person's last thoughts or words? So many torturous questions weigh heavily on devastated shoulders, often for years and years. Is there something that has gone unspoken until now that you would like to say or ask of the lost child, parent, partner, or friend?

The Empty Chair Technique

The Gestalt teacher Fritz Pearls designed this exercise, and I have used it in my work with positive and insightful results. If you try it, you may receive some surprising answers to your heartfelt questions. Place two comfortable chairs facing one another. Sit in one of the chairs. Ensure that you are comfortable, with your feet on the ground and hands resting on your lap. Close your eyes, and bring a pleasing image of your loved one to mind. Imprint that image onto the opposite chair and sit for a few moments in silence, still with your eyes closed. Consider the question or remark uppermost in your mind that has been left unspoken, the question you most need answered.

Open your eyes. With the image of your loved one in the opposite chair still firmly in your mind, ask your question. Let the question rest a moment or two, and then slowly and meditatively move to the other chair. Take a few gentle breaths as you open your heart and spirit, and answer the question you just asked. This may sound silly, but give it a go.

If you have more questions, repeat this exercise. Your inner wisdom or higher consciousness will often provide you with surprising answers, and you may find the peace you seek. It's important not to judge what you feel, hear, and say during this exercise. Be open to any messages that come in, and be sure to say what pops into your head, as that is the way that our intuitive minds work best. This exercise may be even more beneficial if you can record your session with your cell phone or recorder or ask a trusted friend to take notes.

Note

It's no surprise that men and women tend to grieve differently. On the whole, women allow the pain and anguish of grief to find natural expression. Men, on the other hand, are more strongly conditioned against any outward appearance of pain, and they tend to grieve silently and alone. Many, having been berated with the adage, "big boys don't cry," still hear the saying ringing in their ears. Their silent tears are inward, and in many cases they cause damage to the heart muscle. Men will often throw themselves into work and, instead of being available to those close to them, will appear on the surface to be uncaring. Sadly, this tendency often leads to relationship difficulties. As I said before, tears withheld can lead to problems and disease down the road. If you know a man who is struggling with grief, please offer to help ease the burden of his sorrow by simply listening.

Postscript

I was surprised and gratified when Rachel saw Christopher's dog with him. I firmly believe that all matter comes from source and returns to source. It is arrogant and false to assume that we alone hold the rights on spirituality. Any man, woman, or child who has looked into the eyes of a beloved pet has seen the love of God reflected there. I have also come to believe that non-human creatures are sent to us for a specific purpose. Rachel's experience with Christopher's dog provides some support for my belief.

FIVE: MEETING OUR SHADOWS

We need to come to terms with our darkness so that we can live in the light.

Carl Jung

The Swiss psychiatrist Carl Jung (1875–1961) first identified the concept of the "shadow self."His approach, popularly known as Jungian psychology, attempted to bridge the gap between psychology and spirituality and focused on the relationship between the conscious and unconscious mind. Jung identified our shadow selves as the unconscious, negative aspects of ourselves that we often deny, suppress, or attempt to reject. According to Jung, to achieve wholeness we have to first acknowledge, then confront, then forgive, and finally integrate these wounded aspects of ourselves.

This is by no means an easy journey. It can be a journey fraught with fear, an emotionally gripping journey on which we need to come face-to-face with our own dragons, the villains in each of us, our ugly selves. It feels much more comfortable to resist introspection and project those hidden aspects of our beings outward. We would rather keep the genie in the bottle. We can clearly identify ourselves mirrored in others, but we do not often admit that we are the embodiments of, at times, the unfathomable dichotomies between our different selves. If we do allow ourselves to recognize our shadow selves, we often attempt to reject them as unwanted. In doing so, however, we add to our shame burden. In this deceptive process, we become more and more disconnected from our true selves, leaving us captive to shame and negativity. This contributes to our continually and unconsciously repeating negative patterns of behavior, causing our vibrational levels to plummet. If you have ever been in the presence of a certain person or persons who left you feeling "drained," then you know what I mean. Others can drain you. We can, however, literally become drained by our own negative thoughts and behaviors. We cannot neglect and disown those aspects of ourselves without our fearful egos becoming the self-defeating victors.

The truth is that from beggar to king, we all journey the same winding and wounded path toward wholeness. That journey necessitates self-acceptance and self-love. Each submerged particle of ourselves that we uncover, lovingly acknowledge, and reintegrate enhances our well-being on every level: body, mind, and spirit. Our energy levels increase, and our entire selves become more radiant. When we accept the challenge and successfully integrate our dualistic natures, we feel joy. We become who we are.

If we take time to reflect on and examine the patterns we weave into the tapestry of our lives, and patterns they are, we may uncover gold. This may be the most crucial journey we ever take in our lifetimes. Many of the patterns driving our behaviors result from early childhood messages we received that told us we were not good enough. These messages typically came from significant adults, be they our parents, teachers, or others, and they sometimes came wordlessly. Acknowledging, confronting, and accepting our self-limiting patterns and beliefs can transform them lovingly. Think of it as feng shui for your consciousness.

Many years ago, when I enrolled in my five-year training program in Gestalt psychotherapy, I naively thought that as the training progressed, I, too, would progress to the point of being made perfect. All those hidden aspects of myself that I did not like would somehow miraculously vanish. What a misconception that was. When the training was over, to my disbelief, my supervisor declared, "Now you are ready for all those clients who will bring to you the issues that remain unhealed in yourself." As I was soon to discover, he was 100 percent correct. Fifteen years later, I am still learning and growing and remain far from perfect. I now see my life as a work in progress.

Coming face-to-face with the various aspects of my shadow self was one of the most important revelations from those years of training. For instance, all my life I have struggled with tunnel vision. If I think I am right, I can be blind to other options and oblivious to others' views. For example, despite entreaties from various friends, I pursued what I believed to be a potential site for my new home. I pursued it like a dog with a bone for almost two years. My friends could see that the site was not going to work out, but I could not, would not, hear them. They were proved to be right.

In one of the Gestalt group training sessions dealing with facing our shadows, I was almost bullied into repeating, "I have tunnel vision *and* I am okay," over and over in front of the entire group until I could squarely look my classmates in the eye and no longer squirm with shame. That particular exercise allowed me to accept and integrate that aspect of myself and, and though I still regularly stumble over other shadow attributes.

Thanks to the extensive personal work that I have done over twenty years, I know myself pretty well and can now compassionately love myself just as I am, "warts and all." Jung believed that as long as we remained disassociated from our shadow selves, we would continue to attract them to us through outside events and relationships. He maintained that we all are mirrors, reflecting the brightest and darkest parts of ourselves. The ones we conflict with and react most strongly to are our greatest teachers.

During a period in social work management, I experienced struggles with a colleague until I asked myself the thought-provoking question, "What is it I am seeing in this person that I do not own in myself? What annoys me about him?" The sudden awareness was perhaps initially a shock, but ultimately it was very liberating and brought me peace. Ironically, he seemed to mirror my change or perhaps more likely, as Dr. Wayne Dyer regularly tweets online, "If you change the way you look at things the things you look at change." Many spiritual leaders, including the late Anthony De Mello, echoed his wisdom. They were right.

In the following three case studies, my clients, as I did, glimpsed previously hidden aspects of themselves. Challenged to acknowledge their disowned shadow selves, they made positive choices from their new awareness. As you will see in Maura's story, however, it can be difficult to break the ingrained patterns of behavior and belief. Even with greater conscious awareness, we can still fall into the same darn potholes time and time again!

Maura

Following a serious car accident during the winter of 2009, Maura, a thirty-nine-year-old Irish businesswoman, came for treatment. On a particularly frosty night, when she was returning from a business meeting to her home in Belfast, Maura lost control of her vehicle. She hit a tree and ended up in a ditch at the side of the road. With temperatures plummeting to below zero, she was subsequently trapped in the car overnight. She was only rescued when the police responded to the call of an alert passerby who was out jogging the next morning. Amazingly, she had sustained only minor physical injuries, but instinctively she knew that the ordeal had left her body traumatized.

During questioning, Maura painted such a grim picture of her unrelenting, stressful lifestyle that I was not surprised to hear about the accident. I was only surprised that it had not happened sooner. Maura held a very demanding senior managerial post, necessitating regular transatlantic travel. In addition to work-based stress, Maura faced a lot of additional turmoil in her personal life. She had two children under ten, and long periods absent from home caused friction between her and her current partner and family. Maura, like so many people, particularly professional women, was overwhelmed by the challenges of juggling both home and work in an impossible attempt to have it all. Maura, much too busy, was stretched to breaking point. She did not manage stress well and admitted that rather than choosing healthy alternatives, she used alcohol all too often to unwind. From painful childhood experiences, Maura had mistakenly learned to trust no one, not even those closest to her. She admitted that the outlet for her stress was often through inappropriate aggression toward her family. As much as she could see that her behavior was alienating her from those she loved and needed most, she admitted, sadly, "I cannot seem to stop myself. I love my husband and children more than anything else in the world, but I am ashamed that I use them as my whipping boys."

As I always do before I begin a treatment, I told Maura that she was in charge and that if she was uncomfortable she could choose to stop the session at any time. I suggested that she might use a one to ten scale to report any level of pain she might experience. I suspected that considering the most current traumatic event, pain might present itself in the process of healing her energy body. As soon as I maneuvered her right large toe, she reported that the base of her neck was painful and that she was simultaneously experiencing the sensation of a tight band around her forehead. Softly, I asked her if it was okay to continue and reminded her that she was in charge.

"Yes. I see my neck opening, Kate. It's relaxing ... there's a blue light flowing through my body."

As I continued to rotate her toe and ankle, Maura said that she felt each part of her stressed and damaged body respond to the increasing flow of energy as it gradually streamed through her body. A darting pain in her shoulder caused her to wince in discomfort, but as the energy moved through her, it gradually reduced from a level seven to a five and then to a three before leaving her completely. As I manipulated her left foot, the same pattern repeated itself in her chest, sacroiliac joint, pelvis, right hand, and elbow. I assumed that each area where she felt sensation followed by release correlated with the areas traumatized in the accident. The deeper grumbles continually emanating from her mid-region suggested some of the longer held stress was concurrently being released.

As she relaxed more fully, Maura reported receiving comforting glimpses of her grandmother smiling at her. The images caused her to breathe deeper and relax further. No sooner had her body softened in the chair, however, than I felt her go rigid.

"Kate, I can see a woman. She looks like she has a harelip and appears to be disfigured by a stroke ... No, no, it's not from a stroke. Her face ... it's disfigured ... it's disfigured through bitterness."

There was a long pause as I observed Maura's face slowly take on a crimson hue. She took a deep gulp of air, and as her facial muscles contorted, added in a shocked tone, "It's my face ... My God ... Kate ... it's my bitterness."

Startled, I made no comment and gently took both of Maura's feet in my hands. Maura was quiet for a few minutes, perhaps absorbing the implications of her mirror vision. Her breath gradually resumed a more regular pattern, and her face relaxed somewhat. Then she whispered, "Kate, I feel like my heart is struggling to open. I can feel it creaking open in my chest. I can see myself as a little girl. I'm in the back of a car. I can see my grandmother cradling me. I am small. Kate, I feel safe and comforted."

With this new peaceful vision, her body relaxed into the calm of the moment, but then she reported feeling a sharp pain in her neck.

"What is the pain level? Are you okay with that?"

"It's at seven, but it's going away. It's down, Kate ... my neck is releasing ... the pain is gone."

Further pains manifested and then left her body until she finally felt totally relaxed and peaceful. Following the session, Maura said that she understood the message inherent in her experience during the treatment. "I know it was my body energetically healing from the physical assault of the crash."

"What do you feel now about the image you saw of yourself, Maura?"

"Well, it was pretty shocking ... is that really how I am, bitter and angry?"

"Maura, we all respond to fear in different ways. Is this how you are when you are afraid?"

"It is hard to see myself that way, but yes, I do lose it and blame others. I used to feel so angry with my father and his behavior toward me. I think my reaction is how my father used to react to me after my mother deserted us."

Until the crash and subsequent soul searching, Maura had projected blame toward others—her partner, her boss, and even her environmental conditions—for her feelings of overwhelming stress. She patently resisted taking any personal responsibility, as it was easier to get angry at what she perceived to be their poor attitudes. Everyone else was at fault. She disowned and unconsciously projected her shadow self onto others. Viewing her image in such a distorted fashion, however, made her comprehend what she was doing. Compassionately, I suggested to her that when she was stressed, her fear presented itself to others as aggression, which drove away the people she needed most for support. If not addressed, this aggression would affect her closest relationships. Following a long silence, Maura nodded, and said, "I have a choice, don't I? I will drive them away if I don't get a grip on myself."

I nodded in agreement that she did have a choice, knowing the road ahead was a challenging one. Maura's bitterness extended back to her childhood's unresolved pain. When in a state of fear, she lashed out at those she loved. My fear was that she, through her behavior, would create a self-fulfilling prophecy that would drive her partner away. Even armed with her new insight, radical changes were required in order to face, integrate, and heal her shadow self. As with all of us, her journey continues.

Anthony

When I met Anthony, a man in his late forties, he was the headmaster of a large and popular comprehensive school in the north of England, and I coordinated a workshop for his staff on dealing proactively with stress. He had introduced me to his team prior to the training, but ironically, as the workshop proceeded, he didn't remain in the lecture hall. Following my presentation, I was walking down the staircase, heavily laden with my audiovisual equipment and briefcase, when I spotted Anthony watching me from the foyer below. When I reached him, he apologized profusely for not assisting me, saying, "If it wasn't for this damn frozen shoulder, I could lift things." He then attempted to raise his right arm to demonstrate the restricted movement in his shoulder, and added, "This is so depressing."

Although I was due to return to Ireland in the morning, I liked Anthony, understood his vexation and pain, and wondered if I could help. Prior to this, I had only knowingly treated two people with a diagnosed frozen shoulder, my close friend Ann in the United States and a client in Westport. Neither got any relief from my treatments, and not being able to help had been very frustrating for me, to say the least. One part of me wanted to offer a treatment to Anthony, and another silently said, *"What if, yet again, it doesn't help? This man has just hired me to train his staff. What is he going to think?"* Credibility has always been important to me (ego being a part of it, yes). I absolutely believed in what I did as a healer and was loath to have it discredited. The compassionate healer in me won out, and I said, "I just may be able to help with your shoulder; would you like to talk about it?" I explained that I gave no guarantees and admitted that previous clients had not been helped, but I would be very interested in seeing what I could do. I have always been wary of making promises that are outside my power to keep.

After that very weak endorsement for my gift, I was pleasantly surprised when he agreed. The first aid room was a very unlikely setup for our session, but it would have to do, and with the help of an ancillary staff member, we rearranged things in preparation for my work. Had our tables been turned, would I have so readily agreed to a healing session? The answer would definitely be no! As I adjusted the doctor's examination couch, I felt admiration for Anthony in being so open to the totally unknown, and, not for the first time, I wished I could be as open as my clients were.

During the session, Anthony experienced considerable pain. At one point, when I rotated his right ankle, he grimaced that the pain reached a ten. I was sure he would call out "enough." He persevered, and the pain slowly ebbed away. After he reported that his pain had passed, I noticed REM and was surprised. For some reason, I had not expected this and asked if he was seeing something.

"Sorry, I drifted off just there," he responded sleepily.

Assuming he was attributing a visual experience to a dream state, I continued, "But what did you see, Anthony?" Many clients new to my work attempt to rationalize the unusual visions and phenomenon during sessions by interpreting them as dreams.

"I saw a face looking at me ... it has gone."

"Can you see anything now, Anthony?"

"Nothing."

"With your eyes closed, have a look, Anthony."

"I see a face … it looks very angry … it's looking into a mirror … it's gone."

"Did you recognize the face?"

"No … it was a man's face."

I suspected that it might be Anthony's own face—unrecognized and presently unavailable to his conscious mind. I remained silent and continued to work. Anthony reported no further sightings, and I observed no further REM until I reached the same stage on his left foot. As I rotated his ankle in the same direction as before, I saw his eyelids flicker for a brief moment and asked him if he was seeing something then.

"Yes, the man is back … he is looking into a mirror … he is looking so dejected … so unhappy and angry."

At this, the pain returned to the frozen shoulder area, although this time the pain reached a level five at its most intense. Anthony again stayed with it, and the pain faded away. Apart from a few tingles and pleasant sensations in other parts of his body, Anthony had no further noteworthy occurrences.

When we finished the treatment and were reviewing the experience, I asked Anthony if there was anything happening in his life that would cause him to feel angry, dejected, and unhappy. He seemed to react to the question, and as I watched, the color crept into his neck and slowly into his face. For a brief moment, I felt I had overstepped some implicit boundary. Clearly he was not expecting such close scrutiny. With a crestfallen look he replied, "Yes, I shouldn't be so annoyed, as I never really wanted the job. I was persuaded to go for it by my colleagues." He then went on to expand on this remark and explained that people continually encouraged him to apply for a prestigious post in the Department of Education. His peers told him that he was a sure thing for promotion. By the time the interview came up, Anthony was convinced that the job was his. The interview went well, and he mentally prepared for this step up in his life. It would mean relocating, and he happily shared his plans with his partner.

"Kate, I felt ashamed. The interviewing panel thought so little of me … not even a phone call. I thought my so-called friends must have been laughing at me behind my back."

As he retold the shock of opening his mail to find a standard rejection letter, I could see that he felt terrible. All the painful emotion he experienced that day once again showed in his face. He had not even received the usual conciliatory phone call. Although two months had passed since he got the bad news, his feelings were obviously still very raw and confused. On the surface, he claimed that no one was to blame, but it seemed clear to me that he irrationally projected blame and anger on all those who encouraged him to apply for the post. I asked him when he first felt the symptoms of his frozen shoulder.

"Around six weeks ago. You think they are related, don't you?"

"I do not know, Anthony, but it is worth considering."

"You think that face I saw was me, don't you?" He shot back.

"Anthony, often what happens during a healing session is as much a mystery to me as it is to the client, but when you said the man was looking in a mirror, I immediately thought of you. That's why I asked you about your feelings. Truthfully, is it possible? Could the man you saw represent your innermost negative feelings right now?"

"It's possible," he admitted slowly.

"I can't know for sure, but I feel it probably was an aspect of yourself you were not wishing to own. I also believe that today you could connect the effects of your negative thoughts to the symptoms in your body."

Anthony looked exceedingly displeased with this explanation and replied in a frustrated voice, "Kate, I pride myself on being a good man and practice equanimity all the time. How could this have been me? Do I not know myself at all?"

"This equanimity may have actually caused your frozen shoulder, Anthony. When we hold back on honoring and expressing our real feelings, they will eventually find an outlet—either physically, emotionally, or both. Perhaps the very nature of your holding back a desire to 'punch out' has strained the muscles and elements in your shoulder. I admit I am simply speculating, but it is a possibility. Few, if any of us, can be composed all the time. To attempt to be perfect at a cost of your humanness is crazy and, indeed, impossible."

Our conversation drew to a close shortly after this exchange. When he forwarded me the evaluations for the program I facilitated, the footnote on the accompanying letter thanked me for the insight he had gained. His frozen shoulder had greatly improved, and he had resolved his negative feelings regarding the incident, adding, "I have given up being perfect 100 percent of the time. I'm now working on accepting 90 percent!" I presume he had a smile on his face when he wrote the note.

Was it his own face that he had seen? I cannot unequivocally claim that, though I suspect that he received a very valuable insight that day and made use of it.

Amil

I first met Amil, a thirty-five-year-old office worker, in the winter of 2004. The two words that came to mind when I thought of Amil were anger and sabotage. His anger at the world and rigid views of life were physically expressed in his severely debilitating spondylitis, an inflammatory arthritis that primarily affects the spine. In Amil's case, it had resulted in an acutely contorted upper spine. He was one of my first clients in India, and over the years, I grew to know him well. I vividly remember our first session together. It was during his initial treatment that he identified a deeply entrenched belief that life needed to be difficult. It was no wonder he experienced so many self-fulfilling prophecies.

On most of my subsequent trips to India, I met and worked with Amil. He cognitively responded well to the sessions, but in a very left-brained, logical way. Open to my work on an intellectual level, Amil kept a large part of himself closed off to healing beyond the temporary physical plane. He understood the theory, but I suspect deep fear thwarted him from fully integrating the healing available during our work together. He was a classic self-saboteur. He reminded me of the fearful hens on my childhood family farm, with one eye watchful, always ready to squawk a warning for the marauding wolf.

On my trip to Bangalore in November of 2007, I again agreed to work with Amil. By then, all of my clients in India were having the most moving and remarkable experiences. With a rare exception, they were meeting spiritual guides and were either being blessed or receiving guidance and counsel. Conversations with entities that they identified as Krishna, Jesus, Mother Mary, the "eye," or the "old man" were becoming commonplace. I no longer got goose bumps when God came to clients in some guise, just a deep sense of love and gratitude at being privy to my clients' wonderful experiences. Occasionally, I would ask a client I knew well, "Has God a message for me?" and God would, now and again, add something for me. It felt like making do with scraps from the table while others feasted at the same, but it was the closest I could get at this time, and I was grateful.

During this trip, Amil had pre-booked so many sessions with me that I knew he really meant business. I was both delighted and slightly troubled that he automatically thought that the more sessions he had, the better. I have always believed that quality wins over quantity any time. If a client internalizes the healing and insights from even one experience, that is more beneficial than the client receiving a dozen sessions only at a head level. Amil was exceptionally stuck in his head when it came to integrating the benefits of the treatments into his daily life. The conundrum with Amil was that he consistently sabotaged the very thing he craved the most—the acceptance and respect of others. For example, despite knowing how it antagonized his employers, he admitted to consistently arriving late to his work and then, rather than meet deadlines for his employers, he did personal work for others during his office time. He acknowledged that he was in danger of being fired, but despite this, he continued his behavior. In spite of attending the same therapist for years, because of his unchallenged game playing, positive change was sadly inconsistent. His was a classic self-fulfilling prophecy. That is, he unconsciously created experiences that would confirm his perceived unworthiness.

On this occasion, however, my concerns appeared unfounded. Amil used the session experiences to get more honestly into the core of his presenting problems. He immediately identified a number of things that he wanted to work on, his relationship with his mother being one of them. This was a big step for him to take. Prior to these meetings, Amil had painted a sanitized picture of his personal life and feelings. His candidness resulted in a series of remarkable sessions for Amil. During his third and forth treatments, Amil experienced peaceful visions of life deep in the ocean and experienced a healing meeting with both of his parents. These reflected a psychically deep resolution of long held painful feelings. During his later feedback to me, he reported that he "felt good with the resolution." During his fourth session, he also met Lord Krishna, though he did not report any conversation. It was during his sixth and penultimate scheduled meeting with me that Amil had a challenging, but potentially life-changing breakthrough in glimpsing his disowned self. His later feedback reflected a growing inner peace rather than his usual complicated, technical, and analytical response. "I am aware of feeling happy for no specific reason," he said. "Somehow I feel more mature, more like an adult. I spend time being sociable after work, without inner conflict. I saw humor in a situation with a work colleague that would previously have been a challenge for me. I feel more assertive, rather than aggressive. I feel I am more accommodating of others and more independent."

When I asked what he wanted from this final treatment, he said, "An ability to express my feelings, self-confidence, and a feeling of safety." From his fearful shadow self, Amil was predisposed to projecting negative aspects of himself onto others. He admitted to rigid thinking and an intolerance of others in his life. He described his anger as "swallowed often and seldom shown."

During this session, Amil found himself at one point by the ocean. "I see the sea with lots of waves and a stretch of beach. There are large eggs on the sand. Maybe six have been dug up." From this vision he went on to report, "I see an old wooden cabin. I am inside. Outside there are daffodils."

"What else do you see, Amil?"

"I see a mirror."

"Anything else?"

While Amil reported seeing nothing else, the mention of a mirror immediately took on great significance. From previous work, I now expected he was about to see himself in a way he had not before. I suggested that he look into the mirror. Almost instantly, Amil responded in a shocked tone filled with disgust, "Ugh ... I see ugliness. Weird, deformed monster. The thing has no eyes. Left shoulder blade pain. Something happened there. This thing has no eyes, Kate. I see the room reflected in the mirror, but I cannot see me. It's gone."

The image faded for Amil, but its powerful message had not, and I suspected Amil was thinking about it. Silence pervaded the room for many minutes, broken only by deep sighs. I reminded myself that for this, his sixth session, Amil had asked for healing in order to express his feelings, have greater self-confidence, and receive a feeling of safety. From his immediate perspective, he may have felt that he received the polar opposite. But on the contrary, he had just received an insight into the shadow self he disowned. The rest of the session gently touched on his physical being, and he appeared to no longer be open to receiving more.

During our summary of this session, I asked Amil, about the ugliness he saw in the mirror. "Amil, your comment was, 'This thing has no eyes.' What are you not seeing, Amil? On the outside people see your 'daffodils.' Is this how you are in the depth of your being, or is this how you like to present to the world? What are you still hiding?"

We discussed Amil's interpretation of his very challenging vision and his game playing with others in his life, both professionally and personally. Considering that during his vision, his alter ego image had taken on monster proportions, I asked Amil to honestly assess his underlying and unexpressed feelings. He agreed that at times his public persona bore no resemblance to his sometimes-smoldering feelings. So, it really was no surprise that his body was so contorted. As Amil considered all of the experiences we had shared over the weeks, he now felt more accepting that, as he put it, "I play games, but I am still okay." To the casual observer, this may have seemed like a small shift, but it was significant for Amil to let go of his need for perfection. On a very positive front, we discussed the image of the "six eggs" that Amil saw in his vision and explored what they might represent in his life. What was in the process of "being born" to him? What "gems" was he now nurturing? Amil agreed that despite much self-sabotage, his relationships recently had become more open, and he was feeling less judgmental. He experienced more joy in his life and fewer conflicts. Much, in fact, had become more positive, and he had not considered it fully until then.

We make life very challenging for ourselves in our struggles to be perfect. Dr. Wayne Dyer, who overcame personal feelings of childhood abandonment to become an inspired speaker, regularly reminds us that whatever we resist will simply persist.

Reflections

Have any of these experiences touched a chord with you? Disowning the shadow self is like dragging a heavy anchor around. Are there aspects of yourself you would rather deny or reject? Anthony de Mello, SJ, a modern day mystic, taught that we can make choices about the fears and dark parts of ourselves that we are aware of. When the fears underlying our behaviors are out of our awareness, however, they can imprison us. Are you ready to identify those aspects of yourself and honor yourself fully? To reintegrate all aspects of yourself toward wholeness and more joy? If so, the following exercise may be supportive.

I recommend that you record the following instructions and play them back or have a trusted friend read the words slowly and softly to you while you focus on your thoughts and feelings. I use jealousy as my example in the text below; however, you may substitute whatever personal aspect is most important to you at the moment. Jealousy is a corrosive emotion that can unconsciously sabotage us in many ways. It is an unpleasant emotion to own, even in the privacy of our own thoughts. It can cruelly pierce a relationship. The underlying belief that "there is just not enough for me" has caused misery and wars throughout time immemorial. The emotion created by not wanting to share or by craving another's toy as a two-year-old stems from the same root belief as those jealous feelings aroused in us as adults.

Exercise

Make yourself comfortable in a familiar chair. Have a notepad and pencil handy to record your thoughts and feelings after your session. Identify a disowned shadow self that lives in you; in this case, jealousy.

With your eyelids lowered, mentally place that shadow self a few feet away and down to your right (the kinesthetic position[2]) so that you are looking down on your jealous part. What does it look like? Is it big or small? Jagged or smooth? Does it have a color, or a face? Form a picture of it in your mind. As you look at it, get a sense of what this jealous part of you is feeling. Is it anger, sadness, resentment, self-pity, or maybe shame? Name the feeling or feelings.

What message did your jealous part learn from significant adults as a child? You are intrinsically not good enough? There is not enough (fill in the blank) for you? As you look upon this disowned part of yourself, try to get a sense of the love it is really yearning for. Try to understand that love is all it has ever wanted—your love.

Take a few minutes to experience the pain and separation that your jealous part has been living with. Think of how tough life has been for it, wanting only to be loved. Then gently close your eyes while you hold an image of this shadow part of you clearly in your mind. Say silently or aloud, "I am sorry you have suffered so much. Our world is safe now. We have enough. We are enough."

Then gently invite that shadow self to reunite with the rest of you by saying, "When I am fearful, I can become jealous, *and* I am perfect as I am. I love myself just as I am." Repeat this a number of times until you experience a softening and opening of your heart and welcome the disowned part of you back into the fullness of who you eternally are. Feel that jealous part respond to your love and forgiveness as it softly integrates back into your being.

When you are ready, gently open your eyes and come back to the room. Write down what you saw, sensed, and felt.

Please adapt the words in this exercise to suit your particular situation. You may be working with many areas: bitterness, hostility, your judgment of yourself and others, impatience, etc. Identify these areas without judgment. Remember that if we dissect our behaviors and peel back the onion layers, we will find that all our behavior, without exception, stems from a desire

---

2 Looking down to the right helps you feel your emotions more easily and removes you from the left, more logical side of your brain.

for love, and nothing else. We must recognize that two principal polarities exist in this human existence: love and fear. Let's examine impatience as an example for a moment. Remember the last time you felt impatient. Maybe it was in the store when the assistant was slow in serving you. Ask yourself, "Does this emotion not, deep down, when I strip away the egoistic attempts to rationalize it, not have a root in the belief that I am not good enough? Or, perhaps that I will be abandoned?" If we experience love in our hearts, our lives are simpler and more peaceful.

Whatever the presenting concern, you will find that if you repeat this meditation daily for thirty days, allowing yourself to feel love for your shadow self, your negativity, shame, and blame will dissolve. You may be surprised by how swiftly change occurs.

When you complete this exercise, try to become aware of where in your physical body you habitually hold each identified shadow self. This may be an area where you are aware of chronic disease or discomfort, and it may be relieved when you incorporate your shadow self back into your whole self. A secondary positive benefit from this exercise may be the physical healing in the cells disturbed by your negative thoughts. Working within a safe group of trusted others is another beautiful way to use this meditation.

SIX: THE UNCONDITIONAL
LOVE OF GOD

God does not simply preach love; God is unconditional love. Love is the only reality.

Katherine Connon, the Skeptical Healer

One of the great joys of my work is the awareness that God, without exception, loves us unconditionally. I am grateful for my gift and the work that I do, and I know that I was spiritually preordained to do this work. During those early years, I experienced feelings that vacillated between unworthiness and egotistical specialness as a healer. Who was I to serve as God's messenger? Not only did I doubt what my clients were experiencing, I doubted my own abilities, as well. However, contradictorily, sometimes I felt a little too smug.

I am reminded of this when I recall a journey I made in 2007 with Rekka, an Indian client who was visiting me in Ireland. We were in the car, traveling from my home in Westport to Belfast. Rekka, basking in the post-session glow of her new direct connection to God, sighed aloud, "Isn't Kate special?" The words floated over my head like a halo, their warmth resonating about me, finding a home in a small, satisfied smile. Although I would never dream of revealing my arrogance, I did feel special. Who wouldn't? I had a gift that enabled clients to directly communicate with God! Of course I was special. Rekka's words were still comfortably hanging in the air when she blurted out a response that I presumed emanated from God: "She is no more special than you!"

Stunned and rather affronted by this statement, I instantly retorted, "But I am doing your work!"

And just as swiftly, again through her, came the reply, "You are not doing my work. You are doing the work you came to do." Well, there was no reply to that!

Somehow, after recovering from a rather bruised ego, I did not feel slighted by what could have been regarded as a rather sharp rebuke. I did, however, puzzle over his response for some time. Ultimately, it was a relief to let go of the egotistical belief in my spiritual superiority, for this also permitted me to feel less responsible for it. I always felt I was not quite up to the job of spiritual guru, and here I was now being let off the hook. I am not special beyond knowing that all of us are special. My new understanding also allowed me to reexamine and explore anew the question most of us ask ourselves at one time or another, though usually after we hit forty (when distractions, such as college, settling into career and/or marriage and raising a family, are less predominantly in our thoughts): "What is my life's purpose?" I subsequently found mine to be remarkably simple, yet simultaneously challenging.

Many years earlier, I had read and as just as quickly dismissed the words of a writer whose name I cannot recall at the moment. She believed that our life purpose is inextricably linked with what our parents left unhealed in themselves. It struck me at the time as being nonsense. So many years later, it clicked with me. Life would have been easier and simpler if I'd spent it just leaning on my gift, feeling ever so special. Facing my challenging impatience and my erroneous beliefs in a world of black and white and clear right and wrong, to name a few personal confessions, is much more challenging for me. Through the work I do with my clients, the one certainty I have in my life is that I am, as you are, unconditionally loved, and for that I am profoundly grateful.

That may sound like a sweeping statement when you consider those across the world and throughout time who have committed the most inhumane of deeds against their fellow men and women. Were it not for my loving meetings with my clients, I would wholeheartedly agree with you. Through my clients' experiences, I see that God's light shines on *all*. The world may judge us as good, bad, or ugly, but the love of God touches and can transform all of us if we say yes to him. Human beings have erroneously attempted throughout history to show that God fights on the side of "good," when paradoxically, and in contradiction to my childhood teachings, I have come to realize through my work that he is simultaneously on the side of all. That pure love is just too encompassing to allow any space for judgment. God's love for us is the purest and deepest of loves, which nothing can enhance.

The following two clients met God's pure, loving spirit during one of the lowest points in their lives, each at a time when they felt most unworthy and bereft of love. They discovered an unfamiliar God, a compassionate, loving, and humble God, waiting to be invited into their hearts, as he is waiting to be invited into yours.

Tom

Tom had been to see me on four occasions, the first of which was after he heard me speak on a local radio interview. Always cheerful, he greeted me with a happy smile before each session. Once, when he telephoned to make an appointment, he announced himself by saying, "Hello, Kate, this is the pest!" Pest he never was; I loved to work with him. During our sessions, I increasingly sensed that Tom held a part of himself closed off from me. I suspected that additional undisclosed personal problems lay beneath his cheery surface. However, feeling that if he ever trusted me enough, he would open up more, I did not probe. I learned many years ago from an excellent supervisor, Sean Gaffney, to honor and not push against a client's resistance.

In the late summer of 2007, Tom scheduled another session. As I reviewed my notes from our previous meeting in preparation for his arrival, I noticed in large bold type a postscript at the bottom: DO NOT TALK DURING NEXT SESSION. AGREE TO THIS WITH TOM. During his last treatment, I noted from his subtle physiological responses that something appeared to be going on that he did not wish or perhaps was unable to share and that my talking and questioning seemed to intensify this resistance.

As I greeted him at the door, Tom was smiling as broadly as usual, and he seemed bright and cheerful. During the first minutes of our regular review period, Tom told me he had recently watched the movie, *The Secret*. The underlying message of the film—that what we think about, we create and bring into our lives—really hit home for him. Tom lowered his head as he said sorrowfully, "It totally summed up what is wrong with my life. I see everything very negatively. I see myself as worthless."

Within seconds of this surprise disclosure, Tom, for the first time in his life (as I subsequently discovered), allowed his true emotions to surface.

He wept deeply. The sobs seemed to erupt from the very pit of his stomach. In stark contrast to his ever-ready smile, and between wrenching sobs, he admitted that the happy face and cheerful good humor that others and I saw was a mask he had worn for forty-eight years—his whole life.

Now, here in front of me, the mask was gone. In its place was this immense grief, finally expressed in uncontrolled, heartrending sobs. It was almost as if they were being physically torn from his large frame. Forty-eight years of hidden pain gushed forth. He told me that as he drove to his appointment with me, he had decided that it would have to be his last. As he put it, "Kate, I felt this coming. As soon as I entered your room today, I knew this would happen. Oh, Kate, I'm so sorry."

I felt incredible emotion rising in me, and while struggling to resist the sudden tears that were welling up in my own eyes, I asked, "Why are you sorry, Tom? I am so grateful to truly meet you for the first time. I am honored that you trust me enough to let me see you without the mask."

In a calmer but still despondent voice, Tom sighed, "As I was driving here today, part of me wanted to say, 'I feel I am wasting your time, Kate,' but deep down I also feared the alternative. If I stopped coming, where else could I go? I had nowhere else to go."

For the next thirty minutes, Tom described how difficult living with his nickname, "Mr. Happy," had become for him. He had a reputation for being cheerful all the time, and he had never before dropped his facade to anyone—even to his wife of many years. Touched by his exposed, open heart, I told him to ask God for help during our work together. To my utter surprise, Tom revealed, "I saw his face during my last session with you, Kate, and I could not tell you. I felt so unworthy to see him. I shut him out."

That was what I had somehow instinctively known. I wrestled with my emotions as he choked out his feelings of unworthiness between wrenching sobs—feelings that stirred me at some shared primordial level, deep feelings I have experienced many times in my work. Placing into Tom's hands a picture depicting Jesus, a picture that I kept on my table, I said, "Look into his eyes for a few minutes, Tom, and ask him for help."

Tom's honesty and transparent pain affected me deeply. I left the room to give him time and, if I am to be totally honest, to give me time to collect my thoughts and regain some semblance of professional composure. When I returned to the room, Tom looked small and vulnerable. That first intimate moment, when you let another human being see your real self—emotionally naked and defenseless—is terrifying. I knew that moment, could see it in Tom's face, and could also gratefully sense that he trusted me with this new vulnerability.

We agreed not to talk during this session to allow Tom to seek and receive whatever he needed. However, this was to change almost immediately. As I held his foot in both of my hands and imperceptibly started to stretch his leg, I instantly noticed REM and watched Tom's face change. His septum became vividly red, charged with strong emotion. Feeling immense compassion, I softly said, "He's here ... isn't he?" Tom's deep sob was all the confirmation I required.

I took no further notes during this session. As I cradled his feet in both of my hands, Tom sobbed deeply throughout most of the next hour. During this time, Tom met and talked with God. His sobs came in uncontrollable waves, over and over, as he struggled to accept the love God showed him, as well as the love he then was shown by Mary, angels, and an unidentified spirit, who said to him, "I know your story. You need not tell me anything. I will always be with you." Through Tom, I attempted to identify this spirit, whom I suspected was his guardian angel.

Then the most remarkable and profound experience occurred—one I shall never forget. With an expulsion of emotion that seemed to come from the very depths of his being, Tom sobbed, "God is at my side, Kate." He indicated his left side with his hand. "He is kneeling at my side, Kate. He is resting his head on my heart."

I could feel each emotion-laden word being wrenched from his frame. By this time, my own tears were spilling unabated down my cheeks, blurring my vision. With a deep breath, unable to contain my rising emotions, I said, "Tom, God loves you so much. He is down on his knees before you to show you just how much he loves and respects you."

God's humble and inspiring act of love for Tom was the most moving demonstration of unconditional love that I have ever in my life been privileged to witness.

That evening, as I thought about Tom's experience of God's pure and infinite love, I also felt a nagging concern. Would Tom doubt or dismiss his experience back in his world? What if his long-held feelings of unworthiness undermined the memory or even made it just too difficult for him to accept God's love? I thought back to our initial session, when I asked Tom, "What do you want from these sessions? What do you want to be different when you leave?"

His poignant reply all those weeks ago had been, "I want to walk down the street and feel like I have a place here, that I belong." During our last session, Tom had received a lot more than he expected or felt worthy to receive. I feared that, upon reflection, he would not be able to accept the wondrous healing love that God had shown him so powerfully yet humbly.

When Tom called me later that evening, however, I became thankful that my concerns were unwarranted. With lightness and joy resonating in his voice, Tom told me that he felt he had been given a second chance. "Everything is different, Kate—even colors are brighter than before. It's like a bright light has been switched on in my life."

The following week, Tom reiterated how the love he now felt affected his life. He told me, "Kate, even a week later, my heart seems to be physically ten times the size it was before this experience, and for the first time I actually feel it warm in my breast. The laughter I've used as a shield to protect myself is no longer an act. I feel happy."

Tom went on to recount how his relationships with his wife and children had changed dramatically and instantaneously, and he said with a genuine smile in his voice that he now felt closer to them and more loving toward them. For the first time, he sat with his arm around his son as they watched television together. This may be a common occurrence for many, but Tom had never felt able to demonstrate closeness with his fifteen-year-old son until then.

Curiously, one of the reasons Tom had initially come to see me was because of a painful back. His job entailed many hours on the road, and he suffered from lower back pain, for which he had scheduled surgery. Throughout our sessions together, Tom's symptoms continued to bother him, and despite my pleas to give our work together more time or visit a gifted bone healer, I knew he was adamant about keeping his surgery date to remove a disc.

During one of his last sessions before the operation, Tom again experienced the love of God, but this time he was much more accepting of his divine grace. During his conversation with God, I prompted Tom to ask him if he should go ahead with his scheduled surgery, because I wished that he would at least postpone it. When his session ended, I said, "What did God say about the operation?"

Tom simply replied, "My back operation is so unimportant. When I was with him, Kate, I didn't even think to ask."

His response humbled me. He was right, of course. His answer was yet another example of how I continually learn and grow from my clients. When he met again with God, Tom did ask if he should have the operation, and God replied, "Whatever you decide, I will be by your side." God was not taking the decision away from Tom.

Tom called me the day after his operation and told me proudly that as the orderly wheeled him on the gurney along the hospital corridor, gowned up, toward the operating room, he saw God walking on the left side of his gurney, his hand resting on the edge, and he saw his guardian angel on his right. Skeptics would call it wishful imaginings, or perhaps they would say the vision was conjured by his pre-surgery medications. Does Tom care what the skeptics think? Most assuredly not. He made a speedy recovery, and when I last heard from him, he was loving life.

This was a beautiful and defining experience for Tom. Despite being a very private person who was initially anxious that our sessions remain strictly confidential, Tom gave me permission for his story to be told, hoping it might help others. I am privileged to share that here.

Tom met a God neither one of us would have recognized or imagined: a gentle and accessible God, not the powerful and all mighty, the distant figure so familiar in many cultures. Tom's experience shows us that God meets us where we are—willing to offer his unconditional love to help us open our hearts to our own divine worth and grace. Tom's story reminds me of the William Holman Hunt painting depicting Jesus holding a lantern as he knocks on our door. We need only open the door to pure love. We only need say, "come in."

In the next situation, God, as Jesus, shows love and compassion to Amanda, who is feeling totally bereft of love following the painful ending of her long-term relationship.

Amanda

I met Amanda during the early summer of 2008. She was a fellow participant in an inspiring Abraham-Hicks workshop. These workshops are designed to impart the wisdom of Abraham, a group of entities that is channeled by Esther Hicks (abrahamhicks.com). The workshop was held on the Noordam, an American cruise liner, in the Mediterranean. It was ten days of heaven. Everything about the experience was electric—the sun shone every day, and the ship was the perfect backdrop for Esther's inspired wisdom. Meeting and bonding with some of the six hundred like-minded people who gathered together for this shared purpose only added to the pleasure. Sadly, this was not the case for Amanda. The cruise should have been Amanda's honeymoon, but just months prior to departure, her relationship of many years ended, causing her world to implode.

I met Amanda midway through our journey. Choosing to have dinner early one evening, I asked to join her table. Bright and welcoming, with no hint of the anguish she was feeling, Amanda—a tall, elegant, and vivacious blond with bright, intelligent blue eyes—welcomed me with a broad smile. She was a successful corporate paralegal from New York, and she was good company; I immediately warmed to her. After dinner, we decided to meet in the ship's library to work through one of the exercises recommended by Abraham. During our intimate work session, when we each shared one of our long-held limiting beliefs, Amanda exposed a glimpse of her sorrow. It was just a hint, with no details, but it was evident that she was in pain. I was soon to discover just how acute her distress was.

As the days passed, Amanda and I became friendlier. She told me that the cruise should have been her honeymoon. The elegant, romantic stateroom for two had now become a tangible and torturous reminder of her loss. As she disclosed brief details of how her relationship ended, I marveled at the courage it must have taken for her to join the cruise. If it had been me, I couldn't have done it. My instinct would have been to crawl into some dark place, howl like a wounded animal, and shut out the world. On the contrary, Amanda put a smile on her face and joined the happy throng of cruise goers while she tried to process her pain and loss.

On the evening of our powerful healing work together, we had just returned on board from an incredible day in port in Tunis, exploring Carthage and Sidi Bousaid in the northeastern corner of Africa. Having freshened up, we bumped into each other again in the café. The emotions Amanda held back all day were breaking through. By early evening, her brave face gave way to tears of intense grief. Despite promising myself that I would not take on work during my "time for myself" cruise, I just could not help but respond to Amanda. I felt her anguish so acutely and suggested she have a session with me. Due to our separate evening engagements, we had very limited time, but I felt at least I could take the edge off her distress. She made herself as comfortable as possible under the circumstances, and I commenced work. I asked Amanda to journal about her experience with me. Her account follows.

"Hi, Kate! I did my best to journal my healing experience with you. I hope it reads well enough to share with others.

Pain and emotions consumed me when I asked God for a miracle. A miracle that would heal my heart, align me with who I really am, and return me to wholeness. As I lay on the bed, I allowed the healer in you to comfort me, touching my feet. I felt the soothing energy flow through my toes and then move through my body. I relaxed and released and began to see the colors white, red, and yellow—mostly in a circle, with the white at the center and the red and yellow glowing interchangeably around the white. The white glowed and glowed and became the form of Jesus, which I recognized from the images we all know of him. The red encircled Jesus, and the yellow glowed brilliantly like the sun around everything. Jesus was cupping his hands, holding something so very, very gently and carefully, and I could feel warmth. I recognized that Jesus was holding my broken heart, and he was healing it. I felt so warm. I saw my heart getting larger and larger. It was whole and beautiful and brilliantly glowing red with blues and yellows. It glowed and glowed, and Jesus continued and continued to hold it.

You asked if there was anything I was wearing that I would like Jesus to bless, such as my watch. You told me that Jesus would bless things that would remain with us and comfort us when we needed comforting. At first I did not respond, but then I acknowledged that I would like Jesus to bless my watch. I had taken my watch off when we began, so you gently laid it near my heart. Simultaneously, I saw Jesus holding it and my heart, and I again felt the warmth as Jesus blessed my watch and me. He gave me that vision to always carry with me. I relaxed and felt peaceful and soothed. Jesus had performed a healing of my heart.

The next day, I began to release the resistance and negativity that had consumed me. I experienced strong emotions all day, and as I went to sleep that night, I asked God to flow through me and show me what I needed to see and heal. The following day, I started to see things more clearly. I saw that the people who had come into my life were there for a reason—there were elements in them that I needed to see and release in myself before I could experience wholeness. I began to gratefully write down the names of each of those individuals and could clearly see the parts of me that came from each of them … those parts of me that needed to be healed. I felt great joy in recognizing those things and comfort in knowing that all of them are pieces of my healing. That was an experience of expansion."

So perfect, and so like Jesus! He works through me in ways that are always amazing and inspiring. As a child in school, I was taught that Jesus would come again … it is truly wonderful and comforting to know that he never left!

Even in the throes of deep grief, Amanda allowed God's love to come to her quickly and in the most wonderful way. As she experienced her heart being made whole and allowed the powerful energy work to bring her to a much deeper awareness of her spiritual path, I gave profound thanks for the truly beautiful gift of healing I am blessed to share.

I have been in contact with Amanda since the cruise and feel a deep sense of gratitude for having met her. She reported that she was still experiencing the healing energy that she had felt during our session and receives comfort during times of stress with the presence of the blessed watch on her wrist. I get the sense that Amanda has moved beyond her grief, and I can feel her truly beautiful spirit. I know she will always carry her healing vision in her heart.

Just before going to print, Amanda let me know she had met and was about to marry a "wonderful" man.

Reflections

Having read their stories, do you think that Tom and Amanda are special or different from the rest of us? Who among us has not felt the pain of a relationship breakup or experienced a feeling of unworthiness? Their experiences are universal to the human condition. Whoever we are, and whatever our life stories, with their unique twists, turns, and upheavals, there are at least two things we have in common. The first commonality is that everything in everyone's life changes—nothing is permanent. The second is that, paradoxically, no matter what happens or changes, God's love is constant and unchanging. Not a moment, not a heartbeat, not a breath exists outside God's unconditional love, and his love is for each and every one of us. In God's eyes, we are all special. I invite even the strongest skeptic to stop reading, close your eyes, and feel the love of God. As Jesus said, "Why, every hair on your head has been countedThere is no need to be afraid" (Luke 12:7 The New Testament of The Jerusalem Bible), author's paraphrase).

SEVEN: THE PAIN OF SUICIDE

Before the last breath leaves the mortal body, God has already caught you in his arms.

Katherine Connon, Skeptical Healer

Every forty seconds, somewhere in the world, a person takes his or her own life, according to 2009 statistics from the World Health Organization (WHO). This shocking number adds up to over one million people each year. According to the WHO, global suicide rates have increased by 60 percent in the past forty-five years. Suicide is also one of the leading causes of death among teenagers and adults under the age of thirty-five. That number does not include questionable deaths and the ten to twenty million non-fatal suicide attempts that also occur each year. Cultural, legal, and personal considerations affect whether a death is openly recorded as suicide, so the true number may never be known.

Suicide results from many complex sociocultural factors and is more likely to occur during periods of socioeconomic, family, and individual crisis (e.g. the loss of a loved one, economic uncertainty, or a crisis pertaining to one's personal honor). Depression and alcohol abuse are often cited as predisposing factors. The stress of modern life challenges even the healthiest among us. When you are already struggling to survive, life's burdens can feel insurmountable.

I cannot imagine a more painful experience than losing someone you love through suicide. As I was writing this chapter, I had a remarkable dream, a dream that gave me insight into to the bleak hopelessness of those souls who take their own lives. Having never contemplated the act,

I believe that the dream was intended to give me greater insight into the utter darkness that leads one to take her life. In my dream, I could see no way, no light, no love, just an awareness of my being's barren emptiness. It wasn't as if choices, even vague ones, were available. It seemed I was willfully choosing to escape my life. At the precise moment in my dream when suicide became the only way, and I can recall even as I write this the feeling of desolation, there was a grayness, a tiny in-between nowhere space without light, and there simply was *no other way* but death. I could not reach out for help. I could not see how to do so. I was blind.

I now wonder how many souls have experienced this bleakness. How many suffer, seeing no way out? How many parents, friends, or partners helplessly struggle with their unanswered questions, left desperately wondering what else they could or should have done? My sense, based on my isolated dream experience, is that no one could have reached me through the walls that somehow enveloped me. I can only speculate that if a hand had reached into the darkness and desolation of my dream, I would have clung to it as a lost child. I awoke from my dream. Tragically, many do not.

Have you ever you considered suicide? At the darkest hours in our lives, it sometimes feels that it is the only option available. When only darkness exists for you, and all avenues seem closed, and hope is unavailable, to whom do you turn? From such a scary place, when everything is closing in, where do you go?

We are living through challenging times worldwide. The values imbibed in many of us since childhood are crumbling around us. Our senses of self are falling away, senses so often identified by what we *have* and what we do instead of who we *are*. Many people's fiscal security has disappeared and has been supplanted by fear and hopelessness. Before you become one of the tragic statistics affecting many lives across the globe, pick up the phone. Before you make an irrevocable decision that can never be undone, dial someone's number. Before you take the step that will rock the world of your loved ones forever, make the lifesaving call. Tell someone, anyone. Even tell a stranger. Every life counts. You are here, in this sometimes-tumultuous world, because you are needed—despite what it may feel like in your dark moment.

For those left behind, death by suicide can add an enormous weight to the feelings of grief and loss. The late Elisabeth Kübler-Ross, the renowned psychiatrist who dedicated her life to working with the dying and bereaved, identified certain stages of grief that are generally experienced following loss. These stages are now widely accepted as the natural progression of the healing process. Whether the loss is from a stolen wallet, the end of a relationship, or the death of a loved one—the process, if not the intensity, that we all go through is remarkably similar. As human beings, we go through the grieving process many times during our lives. When someone we know ends his life through suicide, the grieving process is compounded by our own feelings of inadequacy, guilt, unexpressed anger, and remorse. The stages of grief outlined here help frame the challenges many grieving loved ones face in coming to grips with their feelings of loss after a suicide.

Following the next sections about the different stages of grief, we will discuss two of my clients, Rose and George, whose experiences epitomize the torment of a deeply grieving parent or colleague in the aftermath of suicide.

The Stages of Grief

Denial

On experiencing a loss, the first reaction is shock, quickly followed by denial. "No, it can't be true! This cannot have happened." This shock and initial denial is a safety mechanism that actually protects the body's energy system. It allows the reality of the situation to be gradually internalized and accepted as painful truth. If we had to fully absorb the ramifications of a terrible loss or tragedy all at once, it could overwhelm or even destroy us.

A sudden death makes the reality more difficult to accept, and even more devastating is the shock of discovering that someone you care about has intentionally taken her own life. That kind of shock can have a permanent impact on those left behind.

Anger

As the truth of what has happened sinks in, we enter the next stage, anger. We are angry with God, society, or perhaps we project our anger toward individuals, such as the doctors, nurses, or caregivers who we think could have done more. It is perfectly normal to be angry when something awful happens. Unfortunately, many close relationships fall apart when grieving anger explodes upon someone who is emotionally or spiritually incapable of understanding what is really going on. Men grieve differently from women. I remember how angry my father was toward me when he lost his health and had to be hospitalized. I knew, in theory, that he was afraid and that his anger was an unwitting expression of this fear. I knew, in theory, that he felt safe in directing his fear and frustration toward someone who would still love him despite his behavior. Others visiting at his bedside were greeted with smiles and words of appreciation. His anger seemed to be reserved exclusively for me. It was, ironically, a confirmation of his love and trust in me. During that period, I felt complicated love and hate in equal measure for the frightened and grieving man my father had become. If you find yourself in a similar situation, try to step back and realize how safe your love is to the frightened person and how much the person needs you. It is not easy, as I know only too well, but your constancy is truly precious.

It is important to remember that appropriate anger is a healthy step in the grieving process, even more so when someone you cared for has taken her own life. Sadly, it is an emotion that often gets buried and deeply internalized following a suicide. Spouses and partners often feel repressed rage at a loved one for leaving them through any death. Unexpressed and little understood, grieving anger after a loved one's suicide often triggers chronic depression or illness.

Bargaining

How many times have we found ourselves in fearful or difficult situations and inwardly cried, "Please, God, let it be a mistake and I will never ..." or "Just let my husband live and I promise I will ..." Depending on our belief system, we bargain furiously with unseen powers in an effort to ensure the outcome we desire. A certain bargaining also occurs in situations of grief and loss. We attempt to negotiate with God. In these conditions, bargaining rarely provides a sustainable solution. It is a mark of hopelessness. We have run out of options, and bargaining is our desperate attempt to regain control of our lives.

A period of grief is not a rational time. Grief is not logical, and although reality is seeping through, we remain in a state that is simultaneously hopeful and hopeless.

Depression

Modern Western culture encourages, and in some cases demands, a "stiff upper lip" attitude to grief. In the West, following the obligatory three-day mourning period, we are expected to be "just like before," fully functioning members of a productive, happy society. In the Ireland of old, we had a much more different approach to death. Typically, once neighbors heard of a death, they sprang into action, bringing food and whatever was useful to the house for the wake—the mourning period prior to burial. The bereaved were encouraged to think only of their loss with the close support of friends and neighbors. Often keeners (people whose task it was to express grief verbally) would attend the house. The bereaved person's job was to sit at the open coffin and meet and greet visitors bringing food and comfort. There could be no denial of death in this situation. I remember as a small child associating the making of ham sandwiches with getting ready for a wake. Death and ham sandwiches were synonymous. The bereaved person wore black for months, similar to practices in the Jewish and other traditions in which black armbands are worn for a year in acknowledgement of one's loss. The rituals of old have almost disappeared in the West, having been replaced with closet grief. In fact, in Irish newspapers, death notices often include the term "house private," and the bereaved are praised for "bearing up" and moving on. Tears have become unacceptable.

In my limited experience in the East, I have observed that many Eastern traditions encourage grieving people to openly express the pain of their loss, retaining a more emotionally healthy, ceremonial response to death. Death, with its resultant sadness and grieving process, is embraced fully as part of life.

After the funeral has taken place, and family and friends have drifted back to their day-to-day lives, a natural depression often follows. This is a time when the bereaved emotionally withdraw from society. Life is no longer going to be the same, and a period of inner reflection and healing needs to take place. Despite societal norms, the time required for healthy mourning is certainly not three days.

During the first year following both of my parents' deaths, but more so following my father's, I would sometimes forget that they were no longer physically with me. I would stop to buy an Easter egg for my father, or his favorite chocolates, and as I lifted them off the shelves, I would suddenly remember with a shock that he was gone. It was a fresh, sharp jolt of grief to my heart each time. Thankfully, as time passed, the tsunami-like waves of emotion that at times I feared would engulf me, gradually lessened.

For some bereaved people, the second year can be even more painful than the first. During the immediate year following a loss, some comfort can be gained from the connection to the first anniversary of the loved one's birthday, Christmas, etc. These anniversaries, although painful, represent a tenuous link to the lost loved one. In the second year, however, life without the dead person can be like a dark void, with an empty future ahead. The rest of the world seems to have long forgotten and moved on, so it can be a starkly lonely period, as well.

Death by suicide holds enormous stigma. Imagined or real, the bereaved have to deal with averted gazes, whispered conversations, and awkward condolences. Within some cultures, suicide is seen as a crime against God, and the person's death is not even reported as a suicide. In these cultures, the bereaved are frozen in unexpressed and unacknowledged grief. Even the word "commit" in the phrase, "to commit suicide," has judgmental undertones.

Although it may seem unthinkable, people bereaved by separation and divorce have said to me, "It would be easier to bear if he had died. It would be a clean cut." When someone deliberately leaves life *and* us, we are left with multiple layers of grief and a ragged sore that may never heal.

Acceptance

Recovering from a loss has no clear timeline. It will depend on the depth and type of the person's relationship to the deceased, the nature of the death, and the bereaved person's life experiences and state of mind around the time of the other person's death. When trying to provide healthy support to someone who is bereaved, we need to consider all of these dynamics. I have a friend whose partner died suddenly from a heart attack. I happened to be in the home at the time and waited helplessly with his partner as the ambulance crew attempted to resuscitate him. It was painful to be there. He left three young children—two of them had to be roused from sleep to be told the dreadful news. When the doctor, a family friend, arrived, I was shocked to see him tip tablets surreptitiously into her open palm as he shook her hand. I was even more dismayed to hear him say, "Sorry—I don't have an envelope." No words of condolence, no sympathetic tone, just words that I interpreted to mean, "Sorry I cannot deal with your loss, so here are some pills to prevent you from feeling it." As Elisabeth Kübler-Ross once said, "If we don't grieve well, we won't live well."

There is no jumping over grief. No matter where you try to hide, it comes and finds you. The stages of grief are like a maze—it may seem like there is no end and that you are not making any progress—but ultimately, the path for most people does lead to peace and acceptance. There are times when medication may indeed be necessary, but it does not eliminate the grieving work that must be done. A social worker by profession, I do not have medical training, but I have witnessed the unfortunate results of someone using medication as her first and only response to loss. To me, it's no different than slapping a bandage on an unclean wound. The wound will fester until it bursts open, causing even more accumulated pain and suffering.

We do not forget someone when he or she leaves us, but gradually the pain lessens. Eventually, most people find an emotionally appropriate equilibrium that replaces the aching hole in the heart. As the well-known Irish broadcaster Christy Kinneally said many years ago at a workshop in Belfast I attended on grief, "We are better or worse following a loss, we are never the same." If you smash an ornament into fragments and then meticulously try to glue it back together, the pieces, like life without a loved one, will never fit exactly the same way again. Life takes on a new form.

The Kübler-Ross stages I have outlined are not set in stone and do not always follow a prescribed order. A person may vacillate between two or more stages until she is ready to move on. Sometimes, depending on the circumstances of the death and the previous relationship, the bereaved person may not fully grieve her loss. This almost always causes difficulties further down the road and is sometimes referred to as "complicated grief." The bereaved who are dealing with suicide often get stuck in any or all of the above stages, delaying or preventing subsequent healing. For instance, shame often engulfs a bereaved person's anger, and a lack of community understanding and support often heightens it. In many traditions, suicide is regarded as cowardly and shameful. In the past, suicide was sometimes treated as a criminal offense. Some U.S. states still regarded suicide as a felony up until 1976 (for example, the former 1958 Oklahoma law, *Okla. Stat Ann tit. 21, §812*, was not repealed until 1976). In the United Kingdom, statutory law permitted that land belonging to a person who "committed" suicide could be confiscated. In Ireland and in some other countries, burial was not permitted in consecrated ground. In Ireland, a person who had taken his own life had to be buried in a *Killeen*, the name given to graveyards in Ireland set aside for babies who were never baptized. The law that allowed for the confiscation of the deceased's lands and demanded separate burial was only repealed in the United Kingdom in 1961 through the the English Suicide Act, which deemed that suicide should no longer be deemed criminal, and a similar law was not repealed in Ireland until the Criminal Law (Suicide) Act of 1993. This prevailing attitude toward suicide only served to promote a sense of misplaced culpability, often hindering and sometimes preventing the healing process altogether of those who had lost loved ones to suicide.

I have worked with the parents and colleagues of those who have died by suicide. The common lament with each has been, "I should have seen the signs," coupled with an overwhelming sense of self-blame. On many occasions, they come to see me only when they have a physical symptom. As I work through their personal histories in the first session, I uncover the emotional trauma that has primed their bodies for disease. It is small comfort for them to know that professional research using control groups has confirmed that there is no sure way of identifying those who will take their own lives.[3] Hindsight only adds to their already heavy load of sorrow. This is what occurred with Rose, who came to see me ostensibly for her diagnosis of arthritis.

Rose's story, which follows, is an example of how the unexpressed emotional pain of loss is exacerbated by our stubbornly held attitudes of old. Rose was my second client, to my knowledge, who met Jesus during a session with me, and it is a memory I hold dear. Her experience illustrates how present and loving Jesus is.

Rose

Rose telephoned me after reading an article about my work in *The Irish News* in 2002. She wanted to spend a weekend at my house in Westport and receive treatments for her recently diagnosed arthritis, which was causing disabling pain in her hip. At the time, I regularly arranged accommodation from Friday through Sunday afternoon for clients who traveled long distances. Rose and I agreed on a mutually convenient weekend.

Rose, who was in her late sixties, looked tired and anxious when we met. She said that she had felt compelled to visit me, as the picture of me in the newspaper article seemed to make some kind of connection with her. She was not the first person to make an observation about that picture; others had said that there was something unusual about it. I had been photographed on a settee in my home; on my left was a shadow that seemed to take on the form of a person.

Rose's initial treatment on Friday evening included my normal information-gathering. During our discussion, Rose disclosed that her

---

3 United States Preventive Services Task Force, "Screening for Suicide Risk: Recommendation Statement," *The Internet Journal of Mental Health*, 2005, http://www.ispub.com/ostia/index.php?xmlFilePath=journals/ijmh/vol2n2/suicide.xml.

husband had died eighteen months earlier, following a long illness. She then told me of her son's tragic suicide on the first anniversary of her husband's death. At this disclosure, Rose's eyes filled with tears, she dropped her head down, and her body slumped lifelessly into the chair. In a hesitant voice, she cried, "I should have noticed the warning signals. I should have been able to prevent his death. Oh, Kate … I am able to let my husband go, but the loss of my son tortures me. I was so wrapped up in my own grief that I did not see his suffering."

Like so many loved ones left behind with unanswered heartrending questions, Rose felt responsible for her son's death. I resisted the temptation to discuss her unwarranted, though understandable feelings of guilt about her son's death. I simply acknowledged her grief and gave her the space to share her deep feelings of pain, brokenness, and suffering regarding her son's recent suicide. I suspected that the onset of Rose's arthritis correlated with her unresolved grief for her son's death and, perhaps, even for her husband's.

The trauma Rose suffered when she went to her spiritual advisor to ask for prayers for her son was at least as tragic, in my opinion, as her double loss. Rose was told that her son was "distanced from God" because of his suicide. Her spiritual adviser described a hierarchy in terms of closeness to God, which precluded Rose's son. I felt her terrible anguish over her traumatic loss and the insensitive and thoughtless comments she had to endure from someone who was supposed to be a source of spiritual comfort and healing. As much as the inappropriate treatment she received disturbed me, I knew she had already internalized the flawed message. My priority became her healing.

Rose relaxed to a certain extent during our initial session. In many respects, her first session was unremarkable; her responses were on a purely physical level. As I gently rotated her ankle, Rose had sensations in her arthritic joints and some relief in her previously painful hip. With her eyes shut, she remarked quite calmly that she was seeing me through her closed eyelids wearing a halo. A number of clients have had this image of me with a halo, an image that would provoke a smile from friends who know me!

I was glad to see Rose relax and get relief from her physical pain, but, to be honest, my heart wanted more for her. I wanted her to find spiritual peace from her anguish. I so wanted to ease her emotional pain rather than just its physical manifestation. I have to constantly remind myself that people receive what they are ready and open for—not what my emotional and spiritual desires are for them. I recognize that my desire has to take a backseat to my clients' perhaps unconscious choices and timing. To this day, this remains a consistent struggle for me. Getting my egotistic self out of the picture is sometimes tough.

The next morning, as I watched Rose walk lightly down my stairs looking so much more relaxed, I suggested that perhaps she would not desire a further session. Rose replied, "I have traveled this far, I might as well have another treatment." I am thankful that she did. Her session that day was powerful and moving and one I am grateful to have witnessed. Initially, eyes closed, Rose reported seeing me as she had the previous, night with the halo around my head. Then, as I gently stretched her left leg, she suddenly took my breath away by calmly stating that she could see Jesus on my left side looking at me. The matter of fact way she reported this astonished me. This was only the second occasion that anyone had announced that she was seeing a spiritual being, let alone Jesus, and I was momentarily startled by the revelation.

I was staring in awe at her prone, peaceful body, watching the slow, steady rise and fall of her undisturbed breath. With eyes closed, she indicated no apparent sense of disturbance or anxiety. Then, with the same outward calmness, she added that she could see her deceased son on my right, also looking at me as I worked with her. Both, she calmly told me, were using me as a channel to her. She added that her husband seemed to be surveying all that was happening from a distance, lovingly observing the scene. Rose reported this vision in an almost nonchalant tone, in the way one might say, "I'll have tea and toast, thank you." I could almost see the tranquility and love in this picture. I could certainly feel it.

Fortunately, Rose's eyes were closed. I was so moved by the grace she was receiving that I lowered my head, thanked God, and cried. My gratitude for her experience made me realize what a gift I had also received by being a part of this miraculous healing of not simply her body, but also her spirit. I was soon to discover that my work, which started with and through the body, was to take me increasingly on a journey toward my clients' spiritual healing.

George's experience was somewhat different from Rose's. George did not intimately know the young man who died, but he was still consumed by guilt, feeling that he should have done more to prevent the suicide. He was wrecked by the feeling that he had let the young man down. What happened during his session was surprising.

George

I vividly remember the first time I met George. It was a warm, sunny afternoon in July 2007. As I opened my door to meet him, I simultaneously reached for his hand in welcome. My smile and outstretched hand was returned with a grim, dour look and a grunt that I interpreted as "Hello." George tentatively accepted my handshake, retrieving his hand almost as soon as we connected. Taking his cold, clammy hand in mine, I immediately sensed the fear he held in his body. As George passed through my lounge, he immediately commented on my fireplace, asking about the materials used and discussing the design in great detail. One would have thought he was there to work on my fireplace—so deep was his fascination and attention. His distraction was a further indication of his anxiety, and after a period of time, I politely asked him to join me in my treatment room.

As soon as George was seated, he said in a breathless rush, "When my wife talked about you after she heard you on the radio, I let it go right over my head. I did not pay any attention to it. Then she mentioned it again. I don't know what caused me to make the appointment with you last week, but I have regretted it ever since."

As he finished talking, he gave a deep and uncomfortable sigh. *Phew*, I thought. This was not the positive introduction I was used to, and it certainly was not what I expected following the warm, though brief, telephone conversation I had had with George the previous week. Ten years earlier, I may have responded defensively or have been lost for words, but I found myself replying with genuine warmth in response to his discomfort.

"Thank you, George. Do you know, I think we should go downstairs instead, and I will make us both a cup of tea and then you can go home."

Much to my surprise, he immediately straightened himself in the chair, tilted his head, tightened his grip on the armrests, and quite abruptly replied, "No. I have come, so I will stay."

I was immediately reminded of the popular Magnus Magnusson quote from the British television program *Mastermind*—"I've started, so I'll finish!" His words were superfluous; his grip on the chair spoke volumes. George was staying. I gently responded, "No, George, if you are here because of perceived duty, we are both wasting our time. It's much better to just have that cup of tea and call it a day."

I explained to George that without his full commitment to his healing, we were on a road to nowhere. Without further ado, however, George, by way of fortifying his position, launched into a lengthy description of his many hospitalizations and repeated attempts to find peace and sobriety in his life. He barely stopped for breath, and it would have taken more space that my recording sheets provided to record the details of his history. The more he talked and revealed of himself, the more I warmed to George. He was a skeptic like me. I asked George why he had come to see me. I suppose he did not know, because he did not give me a reasonable answer. I knew that George, having made the commitment to his healing, would receive exactly what he was open to and ready for.

Despite his doubts, George's session was truly beautiful. Initially he kept asking, "I am imagining this, aren't I?" He repeated this rhetorical question over and over, finding it difficult to accept that he was deeply loved.

During the session, George received guidance on his reason for being here and the purpose of his life's journey. Instead of giving me a diffident, clammy handshake like the one I received on welcoming George to my home, as he prepared to leave my house that evening, he spontaneously hugged me. We had shared a deeply meaningful experience together.

I liked and admired George. He was struggling with many difficulties and obstacles in his life, and as I watched him become increasingly positive, I was happy for him. His struggles had almost cost him his marriage, and even that was slowly changing. Over the ensuing weeks, George received some of the most loving and detailed guidance from God that any of my clients had gotten so far. George was, and indeed all of my clients are, a gift to me. I am unsure of what an "old soul" really is, but George is the nearest example I have found. I looked forward to each meeting with him.

As George arrived for an appointment a few weeks after our initial meeting, his despondency was palpable. He was in great distress. He told me that the previous Sunday, he had met with a young man whom he was sponsoring in Alcoholics Anonymous (AA). This man had marital problems and asked George for advice. George recalled replying, "I can help with your drinking problem, but don't ask me for advice about your marriage. I haven't done so well on my own." The day before our meeting, he was to meet the young man again. The young man never showed up. George did not give it much thought until a devastating phone call informed him that the young man had committed suicide the night before they were due to meet. Stricken, George sat before me, full of sorrow and remorse. He felt tortured with feelings of inadequacy, having not been of more help to his young friend. He felt culpable for his death.

George asked to receive peace of mind from Jesus during this session. By this stage of our work together, George would normally see Jesus and communicate with him as soon as I lightly touched his feet. It was a remarkable connection. On this occasion, however, Jesus did not immediately appear. Instead, with a breaking voice that was laden with deep emotion, George told me he could see the young friend who had just died. George revealed that his friend was holding AA's text, *The Big Book*, tucked under his arm and was smiling at him. George had given him a copy on the first night they met. The copy he had given his friend had a slight rip in the sleeve cover, and he could see the same copy under his friend's arm now, the tear clearly visible. The young man said to George, "George, there was nothing you could do that would have prevented my death. Nothing. My time had come. From now on, I will be looking after you."

The session ended shortly after this meeting. In the weeks that followed, George did not immediately relinquish his feelings that perhaps he could have done more. I believe that a lifetime of mistaken self-depreciation made that difficult for George, but he told me that many nights as he was about to sleep, the young man's face came to him like a guardian angel. He was indeed looking after George.

The comment made by George's young friend raised questions for me; what did he mean by saying his "time had come?" Was it his soul's decision to return home, and is this the case for many of our fellow men and women who take their own lives? For now, it remains a mystery. I have no definitive answers or opinions, only my personal thoughts, deepened more recently by the profound dream experience I discussed at the beginning of this chapter.

Reflections

The young man who took his own life was a recovering alcoholic. It's interesting to note that if a person drinks himself to the point of cirrhosis of the liver and early death, the doctor will not identify suicide as the cause of death. However, the only difference between the distressed soul who pulls the trigger or overdoses and the drinker is time span. The person who drinks to bury fearful thoughts, overwhelming memories, and pain is slowly committing suicide.

Do you know someone who has taken her own life? Are you suffering as a result? Are you angry or guilty? I have worked with many who have been left in pain, and the abiding and comforting message from God is that your loved one is safe, loved unconditionally, and at peace with God, regardless of her cause of death.

What can you do to help those grieving in pain? Follow a child's infinite wisdom. Four-year-old Amit's neighbor, Mr. Gallagher, had recently lost his wife following a remarkable sixty-two years together. One day, when Mr. Gallagher was sitting alone in his backyard, crying softly and mourning the loss of his dear companion, little Amit crossed the garden, climbed onto his lap, and quietly sat there for half an hour. Amit's mother, who was watching her son with curiosity, later asked him, "What did you say to Mr. Gallagher?" Amit replied, "Nothing. I just helped him cry."

The wisdom of the young indeed.

Exercise

The Empty Chair Technique outlined in chapter four may be of help with unanswered questions and unspoken words.

I know, and it is not a question of blind faith, but experience, that our every thought and every word is heard by those who are not with us in body.

I have increasingly found, both personally and through my clients' sometimes-unbelievable experiences, that pain can bring with it unseen and exquisite gifts—gifts that may not be immediately be recognizable as such.

Your pain is the breaking of the shell that encloses your understanding.

Even as the stone of the fruit must break, that its heart may stand in the sun,

so must you know pain.

Kahlil Gibran

EIGHT: ABUSE: THE DIFFICULT JOURNEY TO FORGIVENESS

We must develop and maintain the capacity to forgive. He who is devoid of the power to forgive is devoid of the power to love. There is some good in the worst of us and some evil in the best of us. When we discover this, we are less prone to hate our enemies.

Martin Luther King

"Father, forgive them, for they know not what they do," uttered Christ on the cross. Even as the life ebbed from his battered and broken body, his last words were of forgiveness and mercy. Could we do the same? Could you look at those who have wronged you and forgive them from your heart? A cynic might take Christ's final words and say, "Sure, Jesus said that, but he's the son of God. It's different for me." Not true. When Christ was on earth, however enlightened, he was a flesh-and-blood man, with emotions and weaknesses just like you and me. God calls us to forgive our fellow humans for all injuries, real or imagined.

Philosophers often use analogy to help people understand how a lack of forgiveness affects our physical health. They might say, for example, that hanging onto resentment is like slowly drinking caustic poison. It corrodes like acid, from the inside out. Living with a bitter taste in our mouths prevents us from enjoying the sweetness of the present moment. Deepak Chopra, MD, said that when a patient complained of an ulcer, he considered not what the person had eaten, but what was eating at the person. Is it really possible to forgive someone who has deeply wronged you or a loved one?

I believe it is. No matter how difficult we find it in our hearts to forgive, especially when the one who has wronged us has no remorse, if we want to live well and have peace, there is no other healthy choice.

One of the most difficult transgressions for the human psyche to endure is abuse. Adults who have been sexually abused in childhood grow up with a heavy burden of shame and misplaced guilt. It's hard to imagine any other life experiences that leave the vivid emotional scars that sexual and emotional abuse does. Recent clerical abuse scandals and society's subsequent reactions have served to bring the subject to the forefront, at least partially lifting the shadowy veil on abuse's painful legacy.

I recently listened in admiration to Christy Dignam, a member of Aslan, a popular Irish music group, when in a radio interview he discussed his childhood abuse and acknowledged that it was the reason behind his drug addiction. I was filled with gratitude for his courage. To release his experience to the light heals not only himself, but also those listeners who are open and ready to hear his message.

In addition to sharing his story of abuse with the listening public, Dignam addressed one factor that contributes to the complexity of sexual abuse. In the confusion of his innocent, childish mind—and not knowing that he should try to protect himself or be frightened or repulsed—he actually felt special, special to be chosen. This led to multiple incidents of abuse. Such conflicting emotions for a young six-year-old child are difficult to imagine, but they are so very common. His memory of the abuse was buried deep in his subconscious, as it often is until a life experience awakens the memory. For women, the birth of their first child is often when the flashbacks occur. For Dignam, the flashback followed what seemed to be a chance remark to his father about his drug addiction. Other victims of abuse live in silence and erroneous shame with their painful memories.

The two separate accounts that follow—Maggie, an Irish nun, and Chitrita, an Indian mother and writer—may challenge the skeptic in readers. I understand this fully, as my old friend, the "skeptic on my shoulder," was equally challenged.

In the first story, Maggie was stunned when she realized that her abuser was not sorry and felt no remorse. Nevertheless, Jesus called her to forgive him. As a child, I was taught that God is a judgmental God who seeks retribution—"an eye for an eye" is quoted across doctrines. Maggie's experience gave me a new understanding of what forgiveness really means. We both learned a lot during and following our work together. In her story, you may notice the patterns running through her life.

Maggie

In the spring of 2007, Maggie, a community worker in a depressed area of London's dockland, flew from London to Westport to spend a weekend with me. She had attended a workshop in London facilitated by one of my colleagues, who then referred her to me. When Maggie telephoned, she said that she wanted help with "stress phobia." She was reticent about saying more on the phone and asked if she could visit for sessions with me from Friday to Sunday. I was reluctant to invite a complete stranger to fly from London to Westport when I had no clear idea of the nature of her problems. Plus, I was cautious about diagnosed labels and was not certain that she was open to healing. However, I trusted my colleague's assessment that I might be of help.

When I met Maggie on that lovely spring evening in April, I immediately warmed to her. A petite woman in her early forties, she had a soft voice and the warmest of smiles, which crinkled up her entire face. That evening, Maggie identified her current physical symptoms and detailed her relevant history. In the course of the interview, I was interested to note that Maggie had, on two occasions, injured her right knee, and that she had been having fun on both of these occasions. Somehow, I sensed this was more than a coincidence; and as Maggie went into intimate detail about her past, I realized that she often had resisted opportunities to have fun in her life.

The two main areas disturbing Maggie's peace of mind were an incident of traumatic childhood abuse at the age of seven by a family friend whom we named Robert, and long-standing unresolved issues with her very critical and then-deceased mother. As I have found with a significant number of women who have suffered abuse, Maggie reported receiving medical treatment for chronic gynecological problems.

Maggie said that all her life she had felt judged and bottled-up. When I asked in what way she felt judged, she admitted that it came from her years of exposure to a mother who, as she said, "constantly criticized my every action." The abiding memory of her mother was summed up in one word: critical. When we discussed the "bottled-up" feeling, Maggie surprised me by suddenly disclosing that she was a nun. Immediately she added, as if by way of a warning, that she intensely disliked being stereotyped. Dressed in trendy, bright clothes, she certainly did not fit my image of a nun.

Maggie acknowledged that because she felt "boxed in," she backed away from people and kept them at a distance. She also admitted having issues with the mother superior of her order, Mother Angela, whom Maggie viewed as holding her back from developing her job. She felt additional stress about attending a retreat the following week with her superior. Working with this mother superior was a current source of conflict for her, as she felt her suggestions were not taken seriously and were judged critically. Maggie also outlined a disturbing phobia she had: she was unable to eat in front of people without feeling nausea and panic, a problem extremely difficult to avoid while living communally as a nun.

Prior to starting the actual hands-on healing session, I asked, "What do you want from this session?"

Maggie responded, "To know that who I am is okay. I want to feel a sense of freedom and ease that I am doing the right thing with my life."

With that, I outlined what Maggie might expect to occur during our session and reminded her that she was totally in charge. As soon as I gently stretched her right leg, I realized that Maggie was very open to the process. She told me that she felt sensations in her shoulder and problem knee. She followed this almost immediately by saying, "I see a green diffused light ... Kate, I feel like crying ... touch the hem ... Kate, my right knee is relaxed and easy."

As I lightly cradled her foot, she said, "There's a light coming in through one eye. It's like there are things in my body that I need to let go of."

Her body then gave some gentle jerks, and I observed a steady trickle of tears running down her cheeks. She continued, "I see a gravel road ... my wounds are being healed ... I see myself lying on the road with a cloak around me ... I feel safe ... there is an adult ... like my mother with me ... it's like I'm her ... she is looking at me with love ... *that* was there all the time, yet I only saw the criticism ... just letting me know I am all right. I am sitting up now ... I am safe, but there's still a bit of tightness around my throat and chest ... I see myself at Josephine's [her sister] kitchen table, laughing and enjoying myself ... I told her my problem and heard back she wants to help."

Although some of her observations and comments did not make much sense to me, I resisted the urge to seek clarification and thereby cause her to lose her focus.

Maggie's body trembled for a few minutes. Then she reported, "I feel I can breathe deeper ... there is a warmth coming into my hands and arms, and there is a tingling now in my hands ... the cartilage pain comes and goes and the message, 'protecting myself' is coming to me ... Kate, I can see my knee and bones!"

"Maggie, this might seem a very silly thing to say, but can you go inside your knee and fix it?"

"It's like a little water fall soothing it," she said.

"Can you see what's there, Maggie?"

"It seems smooth. I can't see behind the knee cap … I see myself on the beach. I am in the sea. My body just let go of something."

As I continued holding her feet, she said she was aware of her neck loosening, and then she suddenly said, "The words 'no effort … no expectation' are coming to me. Host came onto spot on my throat, went inside, and became part of it. 'Your words are healing' came to me."

As I worked with her, she said, "I feel like I am a baby being rocked."

As I was closing the session, she said, "I'm aware of the lump on my throat and the words 'Take it easy' are coming to me."

Later, Maggie was quiet and left my home saying that she wished to get some air. I sensed that this session was a little more than she had bargained for. As happens with many first time clients, the impact of such a powerful experience really hits home later. I looked forward to seeing Maggie the next morning.

Maggie's Second Session

Maggie looked bright and rested the next morning when we met in the kitchen for breakfast. As we drank tea, we made small talk about Westport's nightlife, and Maggie reported enjoying a great night's sleep. I resisted talking about the previous night's session, but having observed a quizzical look playing on her brow, I knew she was thinking about it.

An hour later, we met for our second session. She reported feeling much more at ease with herself. During her evening walk, she said that she had become aware, as she put it, that "creativity has to come out of me. I am aware that I am boxing *myself* in, rather than being boxed-in. I always projected it onto others, and I see now that I am actually doing it to myself."

I was delighted that things were shifting for her on an emotional level. She reported with an earnest look that on a physical level, her knee had become much sorer, adding with newly acquired insight, "I feel that my knees are related to my breaking out of my box." I could have hugged her when she came to this conclusion, as I had speculated the same thing on the previous night when she told me that both knee injuries had occurred when she was having fun "out of her box."

When I asked her what she wished to receive from this session, she replied, "I want to be aware that I am more than good enough. To break free—to release my judgments. To believe and trust in myself. To accept myself."

During the first few sessions, many clients take time to reach a higher level of consciousness with me. Some reasons for this might be that clients are afraid of letting go and trusting that they are safe, that it's an "energy thing," or even that their religious conditioning has led them to a fear of this rather unorthodox way to connect with God. I honestly do not know. However, as before, Maggie almost instantly achieved a higher state of consciousness.

As I commenced to stretch her foot, she immediately felt a reaction in her throat, saying, "I see a blue light coming out of my throat ... I see me running toward you, Kate. Kate, I see Robert! I see a rod in the shape of a spiral ... it's in the middle of my throat, and there are two people on each side of me. The one on the right has the face of a boy ... the one on the left is a blur. I am flying about with them ... I see chains coming out of me and the words 'I need to do more of this' are coming ... I see Phil [a nun in her convent] looking encouragingly at me ... I know I am looking externally for approval ... a voice is saying, 'Make connection with your own heart.'"

"Are you taking all this experience into your heart, Maggie?"

"I am taking love into my heart, Kate, and I hear the words, 'Speak your own truth.'"

Then Maggie jerked in her chair, and in a low voice, almost a whisper, as if not to be overheard, said, "I see Mother Angela, Kate."

"Maggie, this time you are meeting Mother Angela from a higher level of consciousness. At this much wiser level, maybe you would like to ask her why she is obstructing the development of your work."

"She's smiling at me, Kate ... she is saying, 'Maggie, you are not ready for this yet. That's why I said no.' She's gone ... I see angels. They are guarding what is happening in my throat."

"What is happening in your throat, Maggie?"

"It's just lit up, Kate ... there is a blue light coming out of it ... the words 'no effort, no expectation' came."

I gently took both of Maggie's feet in my hands and slowly stretched her legs, and then, with a featherlike touch, I softly massaged her metatarsals to complete this session. As I did so, Maggie described little ripples of energy moving up and around her injured knee.

As she did the previous evening, Maggie left the house after her treatment to get some air and exercise. I suspected it was also to ground her energy following yet another powerful experience. The streets of Westport on a Saturday evening are very busy with young revelers, and I had to smile at the thought of a nun out on her own so late at night. Maybe she was going to the pub for a drink? I shook my head at the thought of it. Our final session the next morning was to take us both on a difficult and dramatic learning curve.

Maggie's Third Session

The next morning, Maggie looked particularly bright and cheerful as she reported, "I feel very much at ease. The realization that I have created my own blocks was difficult for me initially to accept, but if I could create them, I can un-create them." She added, "My knees are a lot better, with a little discomfort remaining on the outer side of my left knee."

In response to my usual question about what she wanted from this session, Maggie said, "I want to look forward and enjoy meals with everyone. I would love to meet Jesus. To release Robert. To let the feeling of enjoying myself sink in. To be open to the healing and love of God and allow it to sink in. To be surrounded by God."

As I stretched her right foot, I asked Maggie where she felt the stretch. She replied, "The very top of my head."

"Maggie, is the crown of your head open or closed?"

"Open ... it feels like a little funnel is there ... there is a very bright white light coming into my head through the funnel ... I see a red ball at the bottom of my feet ... it came in first to my knees."

At that, Maggie's body went rigid. For some reason, this caused a shiver to run up my back. Maggie's voice had a tremor in it as she whispered, "Robert is here, Kate ... he said he did not know what he was doing ... he says he didn't mean any harm ... Kate ... he is not sorry ... he has no remorse."

Maggie's body went limp, defeated. The silence felt suddenly ominous. I was taken aback by this turn of events. I have had the privilege of being present to many experiences in which my clients, within the safety of my care, have met and resolved hurts at a higher level of consciousness. On previous occasions, "the abuser," if met at that elevated level of consciousness, has without exception asked for forgiveness, bringing resolution and peace. This was not happening here. As Maggie lay defenseless before me, I mentally asked Jesus, *"What do I do now?"* No insights came, and I struggled with what to say or do next. In order to empower Maggie, I urged her to express her pain to Robert, saying, "Tell him how much damage your loss of innocence has caused and how it has affected your life, Maggie. Get cross with him, Maggie. Express your hurt!"

"I told him, Kate, but he just says he didn't realize. He is not sorry, Kate, he's not sorry!"

Although verbally calm at this point, Maggie's elevated and quickened breathing showed signs of distress. I was mystified, at a loss. Now feeling totally at sea, I impulsively, for the first time with any client, blurted out, "Invite Jesus to come, Maggie. Ask him to help you."

Maggie, to my surprise and utter relief, almost simultaneously responded, "Kate, Jesus is here ... He's saying to me, 'I *know*, I *know*,' in a very gentle voice. He is holding my hand, Kate. I feel so much fear ... it is in my throat. He is putting his hands on my throat ... He is easing the fear. He is now putting his hands on both of my feet."

At this, a powerful shudder rippled through her entire body. "He is now touching my right knee ... now my right hip ... his hand is on my hip. He said, 'Little girl' ... Jesus is saying, 'Forgive, Robert. Forgive yourself.' Kate, I see the little me when I was abused. I am crouching down ... I am unable to do anything."

As this scene played out in front of me, I was confused; my values were being tested to the limit. From my then rigid value base, Jesus should have come like an avenging angel to protect Maggie and strongly admonish Robert. Maggie continued, "Now Jesus has his arms around the three of us."

Mentally I pictured Maggie, the little Maggie, *but who else was there? Her mother?* "Who? Who is there, Maggie?"

"Jesus is embracing all of us. Kate, Jesus is embracing Robert and my little self. Jesus is showing so much love to Robert ... I am telling Robert about all the hurt he caused ... he is putting his head down ... I know he is sorry ... I have to forgive him ... I have to forgive myself. 'Walk tall,' Jesus is saying. Robert is touching my palms against his palms ... he is walking away ... Jesus is saying, 'Some memories have to be healed. We are going to have a great time at the retreat. Keep close to the earth as well as to me.'"

This experience was a powerful and challenging one for both of us. For those of us who aspire to live with higher ideals, forgiving someone who shows remorse is easy. To forgive someone who shows no remorse is far more demanding, nigh impossible. That was what Jesus was asking of Maggie, and through this memorable experience, of me. Jesus asks the same of all of us through his example.

Maggie wrote to me some weeks later to tell me that the religious retreat her convent had attended resulted in great spiritual healing and blessings for everyone in her order; her knees were considerably better, and her eating phobia, except when under undue stress, was gone. A few months later, I received a phone call to say that she had been transferred to another part of London to facilitate a program supporting abused teenagers. With her own healing in place, Maggie was ready to be a wonderful healing conduit herself.

How right I had been about my colleague's intuition! Our work together had taken Maggie and me on a steep learning curve, testing our faith and compassion, and I will be forever grateful.

In the next example, Chitrita, another client, has healing visions of Jesus and her guardian angel that demonstrate that healing can come as swiftly as a click of the fingers, if it is truly the heart's desire. Another skeptic like me, Chitrita raised doubts about her remarkable encounters, and in fact, while she was experiencing visions throughout her initial session, she kept interjecting with, "Kate, I think I am projecting this" or "I don't know if I'm imagining this whole thing, Kate." I had to gently and repeatedly urge her, "Worry about that later. Stay out of your head, Chitrita, and just notice what is occurring."

During Chitrita's second session, Jesus demonstrated his wonderful sense of humor and challenged her about her doubts. When people experience resistance during their treatments, as Chitrita did, this sometimes prevents them from attaining a high level of awareness, but seemingly Chitrita's desire for a connection and her lack of fear were so strong that she overcame any potential block. You may initially surmise, as Chitrita did, that the power of suggestion came into play during her sessions, but when you read the account of Chitrita's second session, this may silence even the strongest skeptic. For this reason, I have reported much of this work with her verbatim.

Chitrita

Chitrita, a Hindu mother of three children from Delhi, is a friend of a colleague. I met her in December of 2007 during my last few days in India, and she kindly offered me hospitality for the few days I was spending in Delhi. She and her children gave me a real Irish welcome, taking me to the local shops to buy gifts for the new home I was planning. I was delighted to be able to return her kindness with a series of treatments.

During my initial questioning, Chitrita told me that she had been sexually abused as a child and that the abuse resulted in her being frigid with her partner, Deepak. She had never allowed sexual intimacy to give her pleasure. She believed she had hidden this secret from Deepak for twelve years. Her story made me sad that such an otherwise loving union was incomplete in this way. Chitrita also said she had a morbid and exaggerated fear of Deepak's early demise. The emotions triggered by this fear, coupled with the sexual tension, were undoubtedly affecting her entire energy system. On a physical level, she suffered from spondylitis in her upper vertebra and various minor complaints. Chitrita shared another issue she was having—one that I was then experiencing myself—writer's block!

When I asked Chitrita what she desired from the treatment, she replied, "I want to heal the spondylitis, heal the abuse, and rid myself of the fear of Deepak's dying young."

Using her bed for her treatment, I prepared a space and commenced work. As I stretched her leg and began to rotate her right foot, she remarked immediately that she could feel a sensation in her upper backbone. Delighted at this response and her openness, I realized that this would be a significant session.

"Do you notice anything else?"

"Yes, the upper part of my neck, where the spondylitis pain is. The back of my neck …" She quickly followed with, "It's in my throat."

"With your eyes closed, Chitrita, do you notice anything? Can you see any colors, shapes, or shadows?"

"Yes, I see something pushing up my throat."

"Are you okay with that?"

"Yeah."

With that response, I sensed Chitrita was thinking about what had occurred. This is common with most clients during an initial session; she was trying to analyze what had just happened.

I gently cautioned her, "Don't try to analyze what is happening, Chitrita, just notice. You can analyze later. Whatever you do—stay out of your head! Just notice. Think all you want later."

To reassure her that she was in charge, should she be responding out of anxiety, I reiterated my earlier words, "If at any time you are uncomfortable with what is happening, just open your eyes and I will stop. You are in charge. All you need to do for the next hour is relax. Are you aware of anything right now, Chitrita?"

103

"Um … no."

"I am going to work very gently, Chitrita. Just notice any sensations or anything else you are aware of visually or through your other senses."

As I gently moved her right toe in a clockwise movement, Chitrita's breathing quickened, "It's touching my heart."

"How does your heart feel right now, Chitrita?"

"It's moving down … it's moved to my throat … there's an itch in my throat … I'm going to cough, Kate." Chitrita then experienced a fit of coughing.

"Are you aware of anything else, Chitrita?"

"No."

"What can you see right now?"

"Nothing."

"Gently scan your body and just notice any parts you are drawn to."

"There's an itch in my throat." At this, Chitrita again cleared her throat.

"Is that something that is familiar?"

"Yeah."

Chitrita coughed a few times, an irritated and ticklish cough.

"Are you aware of anything else? What's happening now?"

"I see orange."

"Don't try to figure out anything. Just see what you see. Breathe in any colors that you see and feel good about. If it feels right, gently breathe them in. What else can you see?"

"Yellow."

"If it feels right, gently breathe it in."

Because I sensed a slight resistance, I added, "Chitrita, you are totally in charge of what is happening. Are you okay with this? The more you relax, the more you will experience. Just allow things to happen."

"Red."

"If it feels right, gently breathe it in. Just allow your higher self to know exactly what parts of your body need the vibration held in those colors. You do not need to think about anything. Just breathe them in very gently. Are you aware of anything else?"

"I see something gray bending over me."

"Are you okay to stay with this?" I was concerned that she not be anxious about this image.

"Yeah."

Chitrita repeated something inaudible, which led me to inquire, "A man or a woman?"

"It's a man."

Even though Chitrita did not identify the man, I immediately felt gratitude.

"Got a hood on," she murmured.

"Do you know who it is?" I wanted to be certain that this manifestation was not felt to be sinister.

"No."

"How does it feel for you right now?"

"I feel the pressure on my head."

"Are you okay with that?"

"Yeah."

"Any sensation you feel, sometimes even pain, is actually good. It is a sign that healing is occurring. Just notice, become a disinterested observer of your own body. Is that figure still bending over you?"

"Yeah, yeah ... he has a beard."

"How does he look?"

"I don't know ... Because of what you told me, I don't know if I'm projecting this, Kate."

She was referring to my introduction, when I had advised her that she might see a spiritual entity. During the first years of my practice, I would begin sessions this way, while trying to be careful not to create false expectations or disappoint a client if nothing happened. I asked her, "Projecting what, Chitrita?"

"I donno ... Jesus?"

I could hear the doubt in Chitrita's voice. "For now, don't go into your head. You can question later. Do not name the man for now."

And now I was careful not to impose any interpretation. "Do you get a sense that you could communicate with this man, Chitrita? It doesn't have to be verbal."

"He looks very kind ... he looks *lovely* ..."

Now desiring confirmation for Chitrita, I said, "Ask him who he is."

With a smile in her voice, Chitrita answered, "He says, 'I am just your imagination.'"

This playful side of Jesus frequently helps clients gently laugh at themselves.

"Is there anything else you want to ask of him, Chitrita?"

"He says, 'Of course I am real ... I am here to help you' ... Oh! 'I love you,' he said."

"Is there anything you want to ask this man ... anything about the abuse ... anything at all you want to ask?"

"I want to live the rest of my life deeply and completely, with satisfaction. He's saying, 'You can have it all.'"

"What about this feeling you have that you can't have it all? Do you want to check this out with him? Did he respond?"

"He's saying, 'That's stupid!'"

"It's stupid?" I almost laughed. Jesus was not holding back, that's for sure.

"He said, 'Please come fly with me.' I'm feeling grateful, Kate."

"Do you want your box blessed, Chitrita?"

Earlier I had advised Chitrita that she could ask Jesus to bless an article, should she wish, if he came.

"Yeah."

"Did you ask him to bless your box?"

When she nodded, I reached over and placed the box on her solar plexus area.

"He's smiling as he's watching me. All that I want is beyond what I can put into this box, Kate."

Then I asked if there was anything she would like blessed for her partner, Deepak. She named a cross and as I reached for it, she swiftly interjected with, "He says, 'There's no need. It's already blessed.'"

Chitrita spoke of her concerns for her partner's stress levels.

"Are you saying this to this old man?" Again I was mindful not to influence her by using the name Jesus.

"I can."

"You are contacting the source of *all* right now. He has no judgment. Just absolutely pure, unconditional love for you."

"I'm asking him to guide me and to protect me. To help me to decide what the right thing to do is. To feel in touch ... to feel together ... to feel at peace. He's saying 'If you feel love, you'll feel peace.'"

"What's happening now, Chitrita? Is he still there?"

"Yeah. His robes have become white, Kate ... He's changing ... I don't know if I'm projecting all this, Kate."

"Get out of your head. Just see what you see. Don't worry about that now. We can discuss this later."

"I can see a place where there is white all around. He is walking down it ... He's saying, 'You can follow me if you want,' but there is something holding me back."

A moment later Chitrita added, "He's gone, Kate, but I feel so, so light, and there is a tingle through my whole body. Oh, I feel so cold!"

The room was warm, and her foot felt warm to the touch, so I ruled out environmental causes. I established that the "cold" Chitrita was experiencing was what I call cell healing; every cell seems to quiver, almost like the body's physiological response to the cold. There is no observable movement, however, and the body feels warm to the touch. I believe that the cells are actually changing in response to the healing that has occurred. Perhaps the painful memory carried by the cells is being transformed. Until scientists confirm this, however, I have only my theories to guide me.

"He's smiling at me and reaching out his hand to me … He's going away, Kate."

With that, I drew our session to a close. As we reviewed what she had experienced, Chitrita again repeated, "Kate, that was too easy. Did I imagine it all?"

I had to smile at Chitrita's struggle to believe that what had occurred, had indeed occurred, but I understood her reaction all too well.

Chitrita's Second Session

The next morning, Chitrita was again torn between wanting to believe and doubting her previous day's experience. Her feedback was very positive, though it was punctuated with the same phrase over and over, "I think I projected all of that yesterday, Kate. It was too easy."

Chitrita voiced what some readers will also question: how am I so sure it is not projection, imagination, or wishful thinking? Over my more than twenty years of practice with countless clients, and drawing from my training in neurolinguistic programming (NLP), Gestalt, and social work, I have learned to know if someone has drifted into a dream state or imagination. The body does not lie. In addition, many clients actually see things they would not, under different circumstances, wish to conjure. Finally, I trust what I am hearing and seeing.

As we prepared to work, I advised Chitrita to be open to what she experienced, to leave introspection for later, to simply report what she witnessed, and to bracket off judgment until our work was complete. This morning, however, was different. Chitrita seemed just as relaxed as the previous day, but as I gently stretched her right leg, she reported no sensations and no visions. For thirty minutes, I went through my standard movements to encourage total relaxation and to stimulate energy, bemused by the stark difference in her lack of response.

I could almost sense a change in the ether when Chitrita cried, "What's wrong, Kate? It is very different. He is not here anymore, and I feel … *nothing!*"

Her words were uttered with such anguish that I immediately felt sorry for her. I was aware of the tension in the room and was considering an apt reply to reassure her when she cut into my thoughts with, "Kate! … He just said, 'Didn't you say it was too easy?' He's back and he's laughing at me!" With that, we both laughed aloud, and the tension evaporated.

Suddenly, I realized what had occurred. Jesus was allowing her to experience the difference between the two sessions. No longer could her imagination or her mental projection be the cause. She was forced to accept that she was communicating at a higher level of consciousness with Jesus—and in such a lighthearted way! His love is always present, but this was the first series of treatments in which I witnessed his humor as a teacher. Neither teacher nor pupil made further comment on the subject. None was needed. For the rest of the session, Chitrita ceased questioning her experience.

During the remainder of this session, Chitrita asked Jesus to help heal her memories of abuse. He made it very clear to her that changing her thinking regarding the abuse was how she would heal herself. As we resumed, Chitrita, once again related her experience.

"Kate, I want to heal the abuse, but I do not know how. He says, 'You can heal that in an instant' … I asked him, 'How?' and he has just snapped his fingers. 'Just decide to make it so,' he says, Kate, and … he is smiling at me."

Chitrita became almost dreamy during the latter part of the session, saying and reporting little. It was as if she had gone someplace else. I continued to gently manipulate her feet and drew the session to a close.

Chitrita's Third Session

The next morning, as we prepared for our last session, I reviewed how Chitrita now felt and questioned her regarding her stated fear for her partner's life. She responded with, "Even this morning, Kate, a thought like that cropped up. But the usual feeling of apprehension, that tight gripping of fear in my heart that accompanies those sensations, has gone. This time

I realized it's only a thought, an irrational fear, and it's ridiculous, so that fear seems to have gone. I don't feel that way anymore, and I can see myself growing old with him. That's a big thing for me. Another big thing is that I have loosened up, so that I feel I can and want to write again and welcome success. I no longer think that in order to have something good happen to me, I have to let go of something else that's good, too."

"You can have it all, Chitrita?"

"Yeah, that was very big for me. There may be some remnants of that feeling left, which will have to go away slowly with time. It *will* go away in time. All of these realizations came to me immediately after the session with you, Kate. And, of course, I now have the feeling that life can be joyful and not full of difficulty and suffering. There is nothing achieved simply because you suffer. There is no virtue in suffering. If that thought is dropped into my head and slowly takes root, it will always be there."

"So what do you want this morning, Chitrita?"

"I want to ask Jesus if I should interfere at all with what my husband is going through, the fears he has and whatever he may be feeling—and if I should, what can I do to help? That's one and the same thing for my kids and schoolwork—should I interfere? What can I do for my husband?"

As is common, despite the fact that this session was for Chitrita's healing, she was more concerned about receiving help for those she loved. I enabled her to refocus by probing gently. "What gift inside of you would you like to receive to support him on his journey? You cannot walk his walk for him. God will not interfere with our lives. He gave you and your husband and children free will. He will not interfere with this. What can you receive to help you support your husband's journey?"

After a few minutes of reflection, she intuitively responded with, "I would like to relax and accept my family just as they are and love them. Support them, and not become critical of them."

"So, for you not to be critical, what do you need to receive?"

"What do I need to receive? ... A feeling of acceptance. Acceptance of love for myself and for the people around me. Feeling critical of others is a big problem for me. I expect perfection of my husband, but we are all imperfect, and we are fine as we are."

As I began my work, Chitrita responded to my customary questions with, "I feel it in my throat and my mind. There's an itch in my throat."

After a few minutes of silence I asked, "What are you aware of now?"

"Swirling round and round … I am looking down at my body and telling myself, 'I love you.' I feel the body is orange. I see lots of knots of tension in my solar plexus."

"What does your solar plexus need right now, Chitrita?"

"Just a lot of love and acceptance."

"Surround your body with love."

"There's a tingling in my arm and left hand. I'm telling myself it's okay to feel that way … it's all right. I see a coiled snake in my stomach."

"What is it?"

"I don't know. There's a burning in my stomach … there's a pain in my left toe."

"What else are you aware of?"

"I can see the hooded figure again."

"Thank him for yesterday."

"Yeah, yeah, I hope I'm not imagining … He is pointing to the pain in me and saying, 'That too is me.' I felt a pain in my left thigh and he's saying, 'That also is me. Everything is perfect as it is.' He's saying, 'Believe, accept, accept.' Still there looking down at me … I have a pain in my heart actually. I asked if I should interfere with Deepak's problems. He says, 'Why would you want to interfere? You have your hands full looking after yourself.'"

We both laughed heartily. "That's so like him, Chitrita."

"Kate! He just picked you up … hugged you to him!"

"Me?"

I felt pleasure and the familiar rising emotion of gratitude as she continued, "He's just tucking you under his arm and patting you saying, 'There she is.' I asked about the boy [Chitrita's abuser] and he said, 'Oh, let go, let go … We are here to help you. Tell you what, when you feel that fear or feel that guilt or feel scared, just hug that fear and know I still love you.' How can I help embrace it and let go … and feel joy?"

"Chitrita, ask him how best you can connect to him without me—when I am not here with you."

"He's saying, 'Write and you will get the answers. Meditate. Anything is easy if you tell yourself it is so. It's like a rock. Most of it is gone. Chip away slowly each moment gracefully.' I ask, 'What about all the aches and pains?' 'Love them and take their message,' he says. 'Embrace it all. Turn inside, turn inside. Look within yourself. Grow in love with yourself. If you are serenely in love with yourself, nothing else matters.' 'I want to grow old gracefully,' I say. He's saying, 'Grow each moment gracefully. Turn inside, turn inside, and look within yourself.' He said, 'feel love.' I see myself as red ... purple ... green."

Instinctively I found myself asking, "Would you like to meet your guardian angel, Chitrita?"

"Yeah ... yeah ... oh, yeah."

As I asked, I sensed Chitrita's guardian angel was already present and that Chitrita could see her. Chitrita—infuriatingly—once again repeated, "I don't know if I am imagining this, Kate. There's a woman in silver flowing robes. She looks very kind."

To maintain her focus I said, "Stay with what's happening right now. Ask her for some communication signal so that you will know when she is connecting with you."

"Kate, she's saying, 'Look inside ... You will get all the answers in good time. Go have fun. You are closest to me when you are feeling joy and fun.'"

Silence followed for quite a few moments, and then Chitrita whispered in a dreamy voice, "My mind just drifted off, Kate ... just drifted off, Kate ..."

"Is Jesus still there?"

"Yeah."

"Chitrita, before we finish, is there anything else you want, anyone else you wish to communicate with?"

"Kate. My hands are prickling ... I see Deepak ... he is an old man, and I am with him ... he has his arm around me, and he's smiling at me. We are old. He [Jesus] is saying, 'Give love and you shall receive love. You can have it all.' Oh, Kate, I feel like crying."

Tears started to trickle down Chitrita's face, tears of joy. Seeing her crying, I let go of my own tears, tears of gratitude and love, as our work together gently came to a close.

Months after our time together, Chitrita reported many changes in her life, both intimate and otherwise. Forgiveness was no longer necessary. In fact, it was no longer an issue. There was nothing to forgive. She followed the guidance she had received, and her writing once again flowed for her.

Mahatma Gandhi said, "Forgiveness is choosing to love. It is the first skill of self-giving love. The weak can never forgive. Forgiveness is the attribute of the strong." Indeed. Any form of abuse, particularly in childhood, has the capacity to emotionally cripple us for life. A certain "look" can still send shivers up the spine of someone who remembers what that look heralded in vulnerable childhood. How many of us have experienced and internalized abuse, subtle or otherwise, in the home or the classroom? The early experience can be so deeply buried in our psyche that we often do not recognize that abuse has occurred. That cutting remark from a significant adult may seem minor in the view of others, but the child's developing self is vulnerable; and it conveys the erroneous message of "I am not good enough."

Michael Jackson's life could have been as full as his wonderful music if, among other physically and emotionally wounding incidents, he had not been told repeatedly by his father, "God, your nose is big." "Hearing that, you want to die," Jackson said in a documentary in his late forties. "And on top of it, you have to go on stage ... in front of hundreds of thousands of people and, just God, it's just hard. I would've been happier wearing a mask." That beautiful person was convinced that his features were mismatched, and he was "not enough." When he died at the age of fifty, he had undergone numerous facial surgeries in unsuccessful attempts to enable him to feel okay. How many teens suffer from bulimia and anorexia because of a cruel taunt about their weight or a distorted sense of self? We can all identify an early painful experience that may seem irrelevant until we explore the resultant impact on our adult lives.

Whatever the hurt experienced throughout our lives, none of us are spared all pain. A time must come for forgiveness. It must be the right time, however, and must come from a healing heart's desire—not from a sense of duty.

Gordon Wilson—Time for Forgiveness

Just before 11:00 AM on the eighth of November, 1987, a Provisional IRA bomb exploded without warning as people gathered at the war memorial in Enniskillen, Northern Ireland, for the annual Remembrance Day service. Eleven people were killed and sixty-three injured—nine of them seriously—when the three-story gable wall of St Michael's Reading Rooms crashed down, burying people in several feet of rubble. The Provisional IRA admitted responsibility the following day.

Many of those killed and injured in the blast had come to honor soldiers killed in action. Amateur video footage of the immediate aftermath horrified people in both communities, and the bombing was condemned on all sides. Among those killed was Marie Wilson, a twenty-year-old nurse who was there with her father, Gordon Wilson.

In an interview with the BBC later that night, Gordon Wilson described with anguish his last conversation with his daughter and his feelings toward her killers: "She held my hand tightly and gripped me as hard as she could. She said, 'Daddy, I love you very much.' Those were her exact words to me, and those were the last words I ever heard her say."

To the astonishment of listeners, Wilson went on to add, "But I bear no ill will. I bear no grudge. Dirty sort of talk is not going to bring her back to life. She was a great wee lassie. She loved her profession. She was a pet. She's dead. She's in heaven, and we shall meet again. I will pray for these men tonight and every night." As historian Jonathan Bardon recounts, "No words in more than twenty-five years of violence in Northern Ireland had such a powerful, emotional impact."

Wilson's words were seen as a fitting memorial to his daughter and to the other ten people who lost their lives because they encouraged a spirit of reconciliation in the area. He was a true instrument of forgiveness, but that forgiveness extracted a huge personal price. Wilson struggled to understand the bombing and the bombers. He came to national and international prominence and eventually met with those responsible for his daughter's death. However, Wilson failed to find his own peace. Although previously a shrewd businessman, he lost interest and eventually sold his business. He was held in such esteem for his gesture and work for reconciliation that he had no space left for expressing his natural anger at his loss. One day, sitting at the kitchen table, his mind snapped. He turned to his wife and asked, "Where's Marie? Surely she should be home by now." Gordon Wilson died of a heart attack seven years later, quite literally a brokenhearted father.

Gordon Wilson's wife later agreed that to the media, he was amazingly serene. Away from the cameras, she said, it was different. In an interview with Suzanne Breen in the *Sunday Tribune* on October 31, 2007, she said, "He would come home, sit down and just wail in despair. Sometimes, he'd cry all night. It was hard to watch ... a big man shrunken by sorrow." She also said that he recited the Lord's Prayer every night.

"And forgive us our trespasses as we forgive those who trespass against us."

Gordon Wilson became known throughout much of the world. Sincerely believing in the importance of forgiveness, Wilson responded to the world's watching media and immediately expressed forgiveness for his daughter's killers. He did so while in a state of shock, however, and was lauded by the example he set for others. Sadly, he did not get the chance to feel his righteous anger first. Forgiveness cannot come prematurely, before the grief work has been done.

What difficult childhood memories have you packed away in a neat emotional box? What painful memories need to be exposed to the light of awareness in order to allow the wounds to heal? Like an unclean wound, the original emotional pain remains unhealed, liable to burst open at any time. Whenever and wherever the injury occurred, reviewing and acknowledging the experience now may be the kernel that starts your process of forgiveness and healing.

Guided Meditation

The following guided meditation may prove useful when you are ready to open your heart to forgive a deep hurt from your past. It may be helpful to record the guidance to play back while you meditate or have a trusted friend slowly read the meditation aloud to you. Ask that he read the words at a slow enough pace to give you time to feel the effects of your meditative state.

Make yourself comfortable at a time and in a place where you will not be disturbed. If you are likely to fall asleep, do not use the bed. Switch off all phones. Close your eyes. Take a few gentle breaths until the rhythm of your breathing is slow and deep. Get a sense of your body as it touches your bed or chair. You are about to go on a short journey, _____ (insert your name). You are fully in charge of this journey. You control all that occurs. At any time, you may end it and continue another day. The choice is entirely yours.

Take a few minutes to find a safe and peaceful place; maybe a place you remember from childhood, or create the perfect place of safety. Make this place as safe and supportive as possible. Perhaps someone you feel loved by, real or imagined, is accompanying you.

Take a few minutes to experience this feeling of safety. As you rest there, look around. See the beauty of this place. Smell the scents wafting in the soft breeze. See the beautiful colors; they are your favorite colors.

A little off in the distance, you faintly hear birds singing a beautiful song[4]. It is not usual to hear this beautiful sound here, and as you listen, you realize that the birds are singing for you. They are reminding you of how loved and safe you are here. Softly breathe in that love. Listen to the

---

4 If by chance you have a phobia regarding birds, substitute a preferred gentle creature.

song they are sweetly singing. It's almost as if the melody has words, and those words are of love—love for you. Softly breathe in that love.

As you take in the beauty around you, you glimpse a figure in the distance. You can vaguely make out the shape of someone approaching. It's a figure, slightly stooped, wearing long, flowing robes. This figure has a gentle, steady gait, and you instinctually know this is a friend who has come to help you. Smiling, this figure sits down beside you and takes your hand. No words or introductions are necessary. You know who this is, and for a few minutes, you remain in comfortable silence.

This loving being says gently, "You have been hurt, and I am here to help you heal and forgive."

As you look at this gentle being, you are drawn to eyes that radiate pure and healing love. You see so much love and compassion reflected there, and you know it is for you. It radiates to you like a powerful beam of light, and as you look closely, you feel that light entering your heart. It is gentle, but very powerful. It slowly fills your heart and radiates out until it fills your entire being. It's almost as if your body is glowing with this light. You have never before experienced so much love and such deep peace within you.

This loving being then says gently, "I know there is someone who needs your forgiveness. Are you ready to open your heart to this person? You need do no more than be willing; that is enough. I know that the act hurt you very much, but your resentment is now hurting you even more. The choice to heal is completely yours, and it can happen in an instant."

You see and hear the clicking of fingers as you hear the words, "Are you ready?" With a warm, loving smile, this being's eyes appear to shine with a teasing light. "The choice is yours. From this place, where your heart is light and so full of love, you can chose to let go of your heavy burden of resentment or not. What will you decide?"

Whatever your choice is at this moment, feel the love and compassion reaching out to you.

Now take a few minutes, again experiencing the deep peace and love filling you. If you chose to forgive, then feel yourself becoming a loving being, full of forgiveness and compassion. When you are ready, slowly open your eyes, stretch, and welcome in a changed and fresh new world.

If forgiveness is not possible for you at this time, do not judge yourself. The hurt has been with you a long time. Just breathe in the love of God.

Forgiveness is the fragrance that the violet sheds on the heel that has crushed it.

Mark Twain

NINE: IT'S GOD'S WILL

Pleasant experiences make life delightful. Painful experiences lead to growth.

Anthony de Mello, SJ

"It's God's will." That phrase is indelibly etched in my memory. I was fifteen years of age and had helped care for Mammy through her agonizing illness. As her frail body took its final, labored breath, and the realization that she was gone from me—was dead—permeated my shocked mind, I started to cry. The priest attending at my mother's deathbed gently said, "There, there, Kate—it's God's will." He meant well, I know, but his ill chosen words stung my raw pain like salt into a bleeding wound. Instead of my meek surrender to "God's will," the shocked priest received the full force of my anger … anger at him, at God, and at the cruel world that had taken my mother from me. If God existed, I rationalized, he was a callous God, a God I had no time or place for in my heart.

God got the blame then and for many of my growing years. He seems to get the blame for so many of our life experiences, from birth defects and cancer to lives lost in a tsunami. He is thanked for the good and condemned for the perceived bad. From the fear and pain that live in our minds and hearts, we create a very psychotic God.

Some years after my mother's death, I was on a visit to my aunt, a nun living in a convent. I asked her, "Auntie Jarlath, if God is so good, why did he take my mother so young?" It was not a challenge. I sincerely wanted an answer. I wanted to understand, to make sense of God. Instead of answering, my aunt ignored the question and said briskly, "It's getting late. You'd better leave. You have a long drive home."

As I drove home that day, I thought, sadly, *if someone who has spent fifty years living a religious life did not have the answer, what chance did I* (then an agnostic) *have?*

To this day, many things about God remain a mystery to me. One thing does not. The God I meet daily in my work with clients does not hang forlornly from a cross. The Jesus, Krishna, Mohammad, Sai Baba, Lakshmi, and/or Devi whom my clients meet has a broad and loving smile, a laughing spirit, and wears many guises. This God, whether manifesting as male or female, in whatever tradition, demonstrates compassion and unconditional love for all of us. Many of the occurrences we attribute to a negligent or unresponsive God are, I now realize, actually a response to our relationship with ourselves and to the natural world. In the end, it is our interpretation of what happens to us that determines our relationship with and view of God.

Managing the day center service for learning disabled adults in Larne, Northern Ireland, was one of the happiest times in my employment history. My staff team created a great place for our clients to learn and develop. The center's atmosphere was full of love and laughter, also providing essential respite for the adults' caregivers.

On more than one occasion, I questioned who were really the disabled among us. The members in our care were loving, accepting, and, in most cases, devoid of the ego angst inherent in the so-called "normal" population. We often had to intervene when our clients' innocence ran afoul of the judging world's harshness, with its emphasis on certain kinds of success and perfection. For example, one client, a gentle, generous, and loving man, came into my office one Monday morning in great distress. He asked, "Kate, why are people sometimes so unkind to me?" He told me he had visited his local fast food outlet the previous evening. On receiving his purchase of burger and fries, he was asked by the teens behind him in the line for some of his food. Without the slightest hesitation, George proffered his food. The teens took his fries and instead of eating, they smeared George's jacket with the greasy food, laughing as they did so. In response to this assault, my staff and I were forced to teach George to be more selfish. We had to toughen him up simply in order to protect him. Sadly, this was not an isolated incident. On similar occasions, clients who had difficulty managing money were short changed by shopkeepers.

One of the most difficult parts of my job as manager, however, in contrast to the joy, was dealing with the pain experienced by some of our clients' parents and caregivers. Over and over, the grief, anguish, and physical and emotional exhaustion they felt came pouring out during our weekly review meetings. I encountered a lot of erroneous guilt and misplaced anger for what those young adults represented, not to mention regret for the past and fear for the future. In my fifteen years of working with these special people, I heard various pseudonyms used for a learning disabled child, such as "a child of God" or simply "a gift." As much as I felt the work we did was special, in those days I could see no "gift" in a parent's giving birth to a disabled child or accepting a subsequent disability. I would never have willingly changed places with these courageous and determined families. In those days, I would have regarded myself as a loving cynic.

Faced with life's challenges, we so often attempt to bargain with God or bemoan, "Why me?" One of the hardest things in life to accept is a problem with one's child. When because of genetic defect, birthing difficulties, or later complications we are faced with the news that our child has a serious disability, everyone involved faces a devastating loss. Upon learning that her child is disabled, a parent may fear losing her sense of self, which compounds the other emotions she may feel, such as the loss of the child she hoped to have and her fear over what the child will possibly face. Instead of the happy future she imagined, she becomes the mother of a disabled child, ad infinitum.

This labeling extends to the entire family system, especially the siblings of the affected child. When so much attention, by necessity, is given to the most needy, the siblings can feel uncared for—invisible. One of my clients, Betsy, lost her sense of self-identity after her son developed autism. Her story is typical of many parents of disabled children. I hope her healing experience brings a sense of peace and acceptance for other parents and gives siblings a better understanding of their parents' emotional struggle.

Betsy

I met Betsy, the American mother of a disabled son, in the spring of 2008 when I was working in Wisconsin. Her son, Joey, had been diagnosed as autistic at the age of six months. Like most mothers, especially those of children with disabilities, Betsy's love for her son was all-encompassing. She used all the tools within her experience and command to support her son's journey toward her vision of perfection for him. When Betsy invited me to work with Joey, I worried that she had more faith in my gift than I and that she would be disappointed. Nevertheless, I agreed to offer my help.

When I met Betsy's son, I witnessed how much love and attention to his development that she, her husband, John, and the rest of her family had devoted to him. Joey no longer demonstrated many of the traits associated with autism. I found him to be a sociable and loving son and brother who had obviously responded well to the family's multidisciplinary approach to his development. Despite all the love and attention paid to him, he remained, however, significantly handicapped by his disability. In the days following my initial meeting with Joey, my attempts to connect with him were hampered by his difficulty in lying still long enough for me to work.

I was a guest at the family home for a week, and during this time, I also worked with Betsy. My initial session with her was unremarkable. As is the case with many who have heard of the possibility of a meeting with Jesus during a session, I suspected that Betsy was rather disappointed that her experience was not more powerful. My standard comment that everyone receives precisely what he is open to and ready for never seems to make a difference to anyone's expectations, even mine.

Betsy's second experience was altogether a different story. I include it in this book because it was the first time in my twenty-five years of social work experience that I finally came to realize the perfection in what I had perceived to be somehow less than perfect. In my previous job, I was honored to glimpse the unique qualities of special human beings. I grieved for my clients when I had to leave my post, knowing they had given me much—I just had not realized how much.

Betsy's experience has been reproduced below as she reported it. Betsy invited John, her physician and pediatrician husband, to help in the healing process. John is a visionary doctor and healer in his own right who works with many autistic children and families at Elementals Living, a holistic clinic and wellness center in Delavan, Wisconsin.

"My session with Kate—September 6, 2008
My session began in the way most of my sessions with healers begin: I was filled with great hope, followed by a blank darkness with few images in it other than black nothingness. Kate asked me if the crown of my head felt as if it was open or closed, and I was not sure, but her work was calming me into a deep stillness, and my "monkey mind" had stopping racing around as usual. I was then guided to ask John to come hold my head.

My head felt as though it were a kite trying to fly in the wind, with nothing to keep it aloft. John's hands helped to calm me, yet at the same time, I was not getting the feeling I wanted. I asked John to move his hands and put one on my forehead and the other on my neck. He said he was simultaneously being told to do the same. Images started flying past at this time, and I felt a searing pain in my intestine, where I so often suffered discomfort in the evenings. John said that he saw Jesus put his hand on my side, and the pain subsided, but then it returned full force. When Kate asked about the pain, I said it was guilt—"Joey guilt," as I had called it many times before.

At first, I did not specifically know how this guilt was attached to all the guilt I had suffered from Joey, but my intestines were aching more and more, and I knew I was on the right track. I then began to see a familiar image. I saw the evening that has been seared into my memory. Joey had been crying for days on end, and I was getting little to no sleep. When a child with autism cries, the anguish is intensified by the impossibility of holding him in your arms and comforting him. One of the main symptoms of autism is a seeming lack of desire for physical closeness. There was no holding allowed—an ironclad rule of his that haunted me. On this evening, I couldn't take anymore. I scooped him in my arms, brought him downstairs to his favorite rocking chair, and smacked him in the mouth, screaming at him, "Shut up!" He bled. I fell to the floor in tears.

This all flashed before me now with Kate. The scene started to play out again exactly as it had occurred all those years ago. However, this time, as I saw Joey rush to his chair, his body started to rise. He ascended and became one with Jesus. Jesus was in white and Joey was in a bluish white, like the color of an iceberg. The two of them laughed and laughed, and Joey was squealing with delight. Then he came back down to the room, and I again saw him crying feverishly in his chair. He was in his chair as I saw him that evening, but it was only his physical body present. It was then I realized that Joey was one with Jesus in a perfect world, doing exactly what he was supposed to do. Joey then came to me with his smiling face and hugged me closely. With a huge smile and a giggle, he went back to his chair, resumed his physical role, tears and all, and then ascended again in squeals of delight with Jesus.

All was perfect and exactly what it was supposed to be. That image of Joey in and one with Jesus is how I see Joey now. There is no suffering, and everything is perfect."

The reader who has had no experience of the devastating pain of birthing and raising a child with a disability may not fully grasp the implications of Betsy's experience. You may say inwardly, "So, what's the big deal? That's what every parent has to live with on occasion: letting fly in frustration and explosive anger and then feeling bad about it." Most parents regret acting out of sheer frustration and, when possible, they swiftly make amends. The emotions of pain, sorrow, and guilt a parent harbors when she has a child with a disability can be staggering. Betsy's glimpse of God's plan provided her with incredible healing from the difficult memory of that painful night.

Betsy wrote the following to me after our work together. It was sent after a weekend retreat she attended not long after our session.

"Now you have to hear the follow-up to my story with Joey. You are welcome to continue telling my story with this part, as I feel it is an important conclusion to my session.

I have been feeling so released of Joey's "burden" since your visit, and my women's weekend retreat was remarkable. I was having a great time with my friend Becky, laughing more than I had laughed in a long time. We even went to a chapel where I saw a vision of Jesus laughing among all the serious prayers. In the workshop, as we went around and gave our reasons for being there, I spoke of breaking my codependency with my beloved husband, John, and coming into my own self-love. I enjoyed all of the sharing we did as a sisterhood and felt my angels and guides very strongly. On the final evening of the retreat, someone started to speak of her son. It jolted me, as I realized that (with the exception of the group leader and Becky), no one knew I had a son with autism!

I used to start every conversation with, "My name is Betsy, and I have a son with autism." It was my identity. I felt entitled to receive sympathy. It was my excuse for everything I did and didn't do. So here I sat, realizing that I didn't label myself this time! I felt completely detached. I was no longer playing the victim. The session with you was largely responsible for allowing me to see my son in his magnificence and to release him from being my burden. I am still in love with my husband, my children, and my career, but they are not *me*. I can be guided to assist my son, but I can't control his soul's purpose. I am only responsible for me. Much love, Betsy."

Many parents will have their own stories to share of the joy, but more often the pain, of having a child with a disability. In Dr. Wayne Dyer's book, *The Power of Intention*, he recalls an incident in the life of Shaya, a disabled child, as told by his father. Shaya's father said, "I believe that when God brings a child like this into the world, the perfection that he seeks is in the way people react to this child."

In hindsight, my attempts to work with Joey were destined to fail. His knowledge of his purpose here on earth probably made any "healing" connection between the two of us impossible.

I have a friend, a father, who buried all of his children after each died from cancer. His faith, as you will read, has been challenged in many ways, yet from a depth of pain and suffering, he managed to reconnect to a loving God.

Mike

Mike is a friend of mine in California. Mike's three children and one grandchild have died as a result of a peculiar genetic form of cancer. Their illness is unusual and is currently being medically studied. Mike has undergone many operations to excise cancerous growths from his face and body. Many of us would, at the very least, wonder at God's purpose in allowing Mike and his close family to suffer such pain. A parent does not expect to bury his child. It is not the "correct" order of life. In addition to seeing his ex-wife die from cancer, Mike has buried his sons, Michael and Gerry, his daughter, Tammy, and one of his grandsons.

When Mike's first son, Michael, died in 1962 at the age of three, Mike was devastated. It took many years for him to come to terms with this loss. It shook the foundations of his faith. It was not to be his last challenge, however. In 1993, Mike's second child, Gerry, succumbed to the same strain of cancer at the age of thirty-two. It was then that he discovered that he carried the gene that had led to the cancer that had taken his family from him. The last vestige of faith that Mike held in a loving God vanished, as it does for many when a loss seems just too incomprehensible and too painful to bear. The natural anger Mike felt in his grief did not pass. Mike hardened his heart against life and God.

In subsequent years, Mike, having lost his sons, became determined to spend as much time as possible with his remaining daughter, Tammy. By this time, she was a regular visitor at Saddleback Christian Church in Southern California. In the early days, services were held in a tent, and when Mike wished to be with Tammy, he had to also spend time in the tent beforehand. Mike told me that he looked upon this time as "a punishment to endure before I would meet Tammy for dinner." Trudging across fields to sit in a stuffy tent was certainly not Mike's idea of a good time.

For many months, Mike shut his ears to the words of the pastor, Rick Warren, as he waited impatiently for Tammy to be free to spend time with him. All he was interested in was seeing his daughter, and this precondition, this forced attendance, was a "necessary evil" he said that he had to put up with.

One very wet, windswept Sunday, having trudged through sticky, muddy fields to be with Tammy, Mike listened impatiently as the heavy rain beat relentlessly down on the tented roof of the church. He then watched in sudden horror as the flimsy roof gave way to an avalanche of accumulated water and one side of the tent collapsed. In seeming slow motion, the congregation became, one by one, drenched with stale, green, algae-tinged water. Mike was mesmerized. Instead of the outraged reaction Mike would have expected from the congregation, he watched disbelievingly as the bedraggled bunch of parishioners erupted into infectious laughter. Mike viewed the hundreds of laughing people, who were by then wet through to the skin, and thought, *My God, these people are all crazy.* Slowly, however, another thought took form: *How on earth can I be the only one right here, and all the rest of these people are wrong?* That single inspired thought was to be the chink in the armor that Mike had built around him against God.

That day in 2000, the hard shell around Mike's heart cracked open, and he started to hear God's words anew.

Throughout his physically and emotionally painful life journey, Mike's love and devotion to God has been severely challenged. He has come through more pain and heartache than most of us will ever have to bear and has become a compelling example of love and faith. His daughter, Tammy, who was God's instrument in Mike's renewal, died in 2004 from the same strain of cancer that afflicted the rest of the family. Tammy held a remarkable faith, as you will read below.

I quote from the order of service at her funeral:

Celebrating the life of Tammy Delin: November 13, 1963–October 12, 2004

Memorial Service, Saddleback Church, Lake Forest, CA, October 21, 2004

The following was taken from a lesson at the Stonybrooke Ladies' Bible Study Retreat on May 5, 2001, in Big Bear. While studying the prayer of Jabez, each lady was asked to write her obituary. Here is what Tammy wrote:

Tammy had a hard life—she knew pain. More importantly, she knew God had a plan for her life. Through pain, some of her family members came to know the Lord, and some are now enjoying eternity in heaven with Tammy. She knew the one way to heaven was through God's gift to all of us—faith in Jesus Christ. Tammy understood the temporary pain and life we now have. Her goal was to share Christ's love with others, praying for their salvation. "Well done, thy good and faithful servant."

This is Tammy's daily prayer, found following her passing, written on the inside cover of her Bible: "Lord, I give up all my own plans and purposes, all my own desires and hopes, and accept your will for my life. I give myself, my time, my all, utterly to you to be yours forever. Fill me and seal me with your Holy Spirit. Use me as you will, send me where you will, and work out your whole will with my life at any cost now and forever. Amen."

The human condition means we are vulnerable to pain and suffering in life, and many shut the door on God for lesser reasons. Mike's faith, renewed through his daughter's faith, is a powerful lesson for us all.

Last Christmas, following a sudden hospital admission and subsequent coma, Mike's life support system was due to be switched off. His close friends waited with mixed emotions for news of his death and release from his challenging life's journey. A dear friend of his from Rick Warren's Saddleback Church sat at his bedside throughout the night that was expected to be his last. It was not.

Mike joined us for a Super Bowl party at my friend's house in Los Angeles on February 7, 2010, tired in body, but very much alive in spirit. A few weeks later, in March 2010, I had the pleasure of joining Mike at a service at his Saddleback Church before my return to Ireland.

Just prior to going to press I talked to Mike. He was yet again in hospital, this time having dialysis. As ever uncomplaining, Mike was looking forward to seeing his life experience in print.

Reflections

One of the stages we go through in grieving, as discussed in chapter six, is anger. Anger is a natural expression of loss. In many years of working closely with parents and caregivers, I have found that some people become stuck in this stage of grieving—including some parents of children with disabilities. The entire process of giving birth to a new child should be a joyous occasion, one for celebration. Having a child with a disability can turn a joyous experience into a desperate and lonely sadness, one that a parent is often not encouraged to express openly. Instead, others judiciously ignore the disability or offer inept platitudes to conceal their discomfort. Their comments, such as "God has sent you a little angel," do not help. She did not want an angel, she wanted a "perfect" baby who would eventually grow up, possibly marry, have children, and be independent. A dissonance of feelings abounds, and the only "safe" and socially acceptable one is anger. It is no compensation to know that the service industry for this "customer base" has grown, propelled by the angry emotions of the frustrated and grieving caregivers. Sadly, however, regardless of who benefits from the products and services, in the long run the caregiver is all too often left with "complicated" or unresolved grief.

As with Betsy, Mike's life was turned upside down and inside out with so many personal losses. For many years, Mike turned his feelings of grief inward, contributing, no doubt, to the difficulties he encountered in life. It is hard to imagine a loving God in this scenario, yet Mike found him in the depths of his pain and, crucially, let him in. This is a God of pure love who is with us each and every painful step, a God we will comprehend completely in time.

Do you recognize yourself or someone you care about in these examples? If Betsy's or Mike's experience has touched a chord in your life, I would encourage you to take a few minutes to acknowledge your feelings when you have time to be at peace.

Do you have a child with a disability? Have you experienced the tragic loss of someone close to you through death, long-term disability, or illness? How has it affected the other close relationships in your life? Are you angry, sad, frustrated, or depressed? How has it impacted your relationship with God?

The following exercise may be of help:

Take a moment to remember the day your loved one was born or developed a disability. What were your feelings that day? I am sure they are etched deeply in your memory. Write them down. For a range of reasons, these feelings are often left unacknowledged, sometimes for years or even for a lifetime. Left unacknowledged, they can cause silent havoc. Take some time with this, and if possible, discuss these feelings with a trusted friend.

Now consider for a few moments the reality that your loved one is perfect in the eyes of God and that he or she is in a perfect place in creation. See your loved one as Betsy saw Joey, one with God and in total perfection. Up until now, you could only see a fragment of life's bigger picture for you and your loved one—love tinged with anguish, the fear for the future, and perhaps even unresolved grief and anger. Now, for a few minutes and with different eyes, allow your perspective to change. This kind of "tragedy" is often more agonizing for the caregiver than the loved one. Your road is the tougher one. At this moment, what is it that requires healing *in you*? I know this is difficult, but please try. Have you lost your identity, as Betsy had for many years? What do you need to do to reclaim yours? There is not a single piece in your life's jigsaw puzzle that does not fit, not one single piece. Maybe right now you are too close to the fragments to see the perfect pattern. What do you need to do to reach inner peace? As you read these words, let a different possibility filter through. You are in God's capable and loving arms.

Coming from a service background, I realize that support services, particularly respite, are inadequate. It can be helpful and healing to start a support group in the neighborhood, or start an informal respite service among other caregivers. What practical and emotional support can you build for yourself and the significant others in your life?

We can see only a fraction of the big picture that makes up our truly magnificent lives. When we are faced with an enormous challenge, such as raising a child with disabilities or coping with the altered persona of a loved one, it may be helpful to remember that we are all perfect, in every moment, in the eyes of God.

If you knew who walked beside you at all times on this path you have chosen, you could never experience fear again.

Helen Schucman and William Thetford, A Course in Miracles

TEN: PAST, PRESENT, AND FUTURE

Time is not at all what it seems. It does not flow in only one direction, and the future exists simultaneously with the past.

Albert Einstein

Because this is the most challenging chapter, I have intentionally placed it at the end of the book. Throughout the last ten years of my amazing journey as a healer, my understanding of reality has radically shifted, and it continues to expand to this day. Despite my skepticism and occasional astonishment at what my clients were experiencing, at some level, I always knew that I was witnessing truth. Indeed, from the beginning of my personal search for answers, I have been gently and surely guided, and I know that the journey is far from over. In this time of expanding light, we are all being called to open our eyes, hearts, and minds in order to embrace a higher vision of the world around us and ourselves. I say this because the chapter you are now in the process of reading may challenge you, as it initially did me.

We live in a world that runs on linear time. As children, we learn how to tell time and then allow it to frame the rest of our lives. Years ago, small children used to be exempt from its reach, but modern society has gobbled up the unstructured abandon some of us remember from our childhood. The fabric of life is impossible to imagine without the clock. My late father drummed the responsibility into his children to always be on time, and I am fastidious to the point of obsessive about never being late to anything.

I remember long, hot summers that seemed to last forever from my youth, and when grown-ups complained that time sped up as they got older, I had no concept of what they were talking about. Now everything goes by in a flash.

When I was a child, time travel was the stuff of science fiction and mad scientists. I still remember the TV show about Dr. Who and his time machine, the Tardis. I find it fascinating that groundbreaking research in quantum mechanics and physics is bridging the gap between the science fiction version of time from my youth and the complex theories of time that are now floating into mainstream consciousness. As far back as the early 1900s, Einstein said, "The distinction between past, present, and future is only a stubbornly held illusion." Some of my clients' experiences certainly validate this expanded view of time and have forced me to reexamine what I believe to be true about the time-space continuum.

The following astounding encounters that my client, Ghouse, experienced while we worked together in India in 2006 did not shock me as much as my experiences with Róisín had back in 1999. When Róisín announced that she saw a smiling Jesus and frightened me so much, she was preparing me for what has turned out to be a remarkable journey.

You have had less time than I to absorb what unfolds in this book. A long time ago, I was forced to let go of my need to control and rationalize my clients' experiences, and I have no theory to explain the experience you will read here. Greater minds than mine have struggled to prove what they "knew." Even Albert Einstein had this struggle, and many people still do today.

Ghouse

During Christmas in 2006, I stayed with friends in Bangalore, which is in the mid-south of India. Rekka, a psychologist colleague, had arranged for me to work with some of her clients during my weeklong visit. In fact, this was my third visit to Bangalore, and each time I had had the opportunity to work with her clients. This was always a real pleasure. Without exception, they were all perceptive and self-aware. As a result, it was rewarding and straightforward to work with them.

During my initial visit to Bangalore, Rekka suggested that I see clients for a prearranged package of three sessions. She reasoned that it would encourage them to focus on and work through their problems. It meant I would see fewer clients during my visit, but conversely, this arrangement meant I might be able to help the clients I did see achieve deeper and fuller understanding and resolution of their present issues.

Rekka was right. I had the pleasure of being part of these clients' healing journeys. Each session enriched the next, deepening and consolidating the positive changes. This has been the method of my work ever since.

As usual, Rekka had generously provided me with her office for my work with her clients. During this visit, she asked me to meet Ghouse, a businessman based in Pune who was visiting his family in Bangalore for Christmas. Ghouse was not a client; he was a person she knew socially. His mother had died the previous January. Rekka was concerned that he had not grieved fully for her. Because Geeta, his wife, was her colleague, Rekka felt that she could not suggest counseling Ghouse personally.

That first morning, as I walked through the gate to the treatment center where Rekka had her office, a voice greeted me with, "Hello, I am early. Is that okay?" I turned and met his dark eyes. Mohammad Ghouse was tall, well built, and around thirty years old, or so I guessed. While attractive, his face held no trace of a smile. As he walked toward me, his labored movements spoke volumes of carried grief. Immediately, I was drawn again to the look in his eyes. Listless and sad, he appeared to be full of wariness and unshed tears. *He's on guard*, I thought briefly. *Does he really want to be here?* His punctuality said yes, but his body language said no. I held out my hand, saying, "I am so pleased to meet you, Ghouse." He shook my hand, met my eyes for a brief moment, and smiled slightly, but he did not reply. The smile did not reach his eyes. I could sense his ambiguity.

I led the way toward the center, and as we entered the building together, I asked the silent Ghouse to wait a moment as I prepared my workplace. Preparing the room meant going through the motions of plugging in the ineffectual mosquito repellent and turning on the inadequate electric fan. The fan's purpose was not only to escape the incessant Indian heat, but also to deter the mosquitoes that were now delighted to see me. Even with windows tightly closed, mosquitoes would lurk in dark corners or behind curtains, waiting to emerge for my blood. If I positioned myself directly below the ceiling fan while I was working, I just might escape a few bites. Perhaps it was my Irish skin, but I did, unfortunately, seem to attract the most determined, bloodthirsty mosquitoes in all of India.

Taking my recording sheets from my case, I called Ghouse into the room and asked him to sit with me at the desk while I took notes. I motioned for him to take the comfortable high backed padded office chair, while I sat in the cane chair at the side of the desk. If possible, I have always ensured that my clients sit in the "master" chair to immediately signal that they are in charge. Sessions can seem daunting to someone new to the experience, and the non-verbal message right from the onset that the client is in control is of the utmost importance.

I was acutely aware of Ghouse's body language: his arms tightly folded across his large frame while he leaned slightly away from me; his breathing shallow and fast ... he was physically present, but he was not with me. Once again, I sensed resistance and thought that the session was not going to be an easy one for either of us.

As always, I began by taking a personal history. Although Ghouse was a stranger, I had previously been introduced to Geeta, his wife, so I made a point of placing an additional emphasis on strict confidentiality. I was surprised to discover that he was actually more open than his non-verbal communication had suggested, and he quickly identified the main unease in his life. "Frustration," he said flatly. "Things are not working out for me."

He and his wife had been unable to find a house to live in, despite "actively seeking" one for eighteen months. Either he or his wife would find something wrong with each prospective property. We discussed possible blocks that might be preventing their finding a suitable new home and ways to accommodate the finding of an acceptable choice. As we continued, Ghouse became visibly more relaxed, leaning forward as we spoke, his breathing slower and deeper in his belly. His eyes had lost the wary look; I sensed that we had gained rapport.

He then told me of the significant losses in his life and how the loss of his mother the previous January still affected him. He admitted that he "could not let her go." With her death, he had lost his principle support system, and then, with such a depth of sadness, he said, "I just cannot accept her death."

What a wrenching admission from a man who described himself as aloof. He was obviously feeling deep loss, and yet there was no outward sign of emotion beyond the transparent pain in his eyes.

When I questioned Ghouse about his daily routines, he told me that his sleeping pattern was poor. He would spend at least one hour every night ruminating over current issues, always choosing a negative perspective on every event. Under pressure, he would lose his focus; when stressed, he would lose confidence in his ability to cope, and he would feel dejected.

His work would suffer. Many nights he would lay awake, sometimes watching television, as his wife slept.

On two occasions, Ghouse remembered a recurring dream that was possibly related to the loss of his mother and his inability to grieve. He described seeing a "deep well that has no water in it, but rather is full of snakes." I resisted the temptation to discuss the content and merely recorded and bracketed off the information. My question about his desires for the session, elicited this response: "I want to feel secure, feel lighter, and feel confident even in the midst of stress." Then, much to my surprise, he softly and without hesitation added, "I want to say goodbye to Ma."

The pained look on his face as he said these poignant words touched me. He knew he had to let go. He was ready, but truth be told, in his heart he was afraid. What would be left if he let go? Ghouse had no questions for me regarding the work. I explained the process that I would be using for his treatment and stressed that if anything bothered him during it, he could open his eyes at any time and ask me to stop.

I began gently. During the first movements, Ghouse described quite strong pain in his stomach and colon; these pains reduced as I worked, and then they dissipated. Suddenly, his body gave a slight but significant jerk, and he said, "I felt a sort of shock in this area," pointing to his heart. I noticed some REM, and his head moved slightly, as if he were trying to follow something.

"With your eyes closed, Ghouse, do you see anything?"

"I see a white ball of light about the size of a tennis ball, oscillating … it is hitting something and now going through it … a green colored candle with a glass holder … a dish … I see Jesus on the cross … two ladies and children are praying … I don't see their faces … don't know them … I can see Christ's face."

"What does he look like, Ghouse?"

"He looks as if he is blessing the ladies and children. I see a full moon … I am seeing two things … I see Christ on the cross on my right, and on my left, in another place, I see an object I am not able to recognize … it is like a small stick thing. Below Christ, I see an alphabet in a different language."

"Do you know what language this is, Ghouse?"

"I do not recognize it … it has gone … I see a dark night, a mountain, a long road … I am seeing the other side of the mountain now from the other side … it is *very* deep, *very* deep … a small waterfall falls through the mountain … not much water—*very* deep … bushes this side of the mountain … I see an old man sitting … he has a beard, looking very calm, with a big stick … I am seeing this from on top."

I tried to keep the conversation flowing. "Where are you now, Ghouse?"

"I am looking down on him … he has a blanket around his shoulders … I am getting a pain in my chest!"

"What number is the pain, Ghouse?"

"It's an eight."

In a reassuring voice I softly inquired, "Are you okay to stay with it, Ghouse?"

"Yes."

I worked gently, to encourage healing energy to clear the blockage and reduce the pain. "What number is the pain now, Ghouse?"

"A three. The pain is in my back now."

"What number is the pain, Ghouse?"

"Seven."

I asked if he could stay with it, and he said yes. My movements were barely discernable. "What is the pain now, Ghouse?"

"Three. The pain is in my stomach."

I kept working. "What is the pain now, Ghouse?"

He did not respond to my question, instead saying, "I see the old man. He got up … he sees me … he is asking me to come down."

"Are you going down, Ghouse?"

"I am unable to do it … he is asking me to come down again."

"Ask the old man to help you, Ghouse."

"I am going down … I am holding his hand in both of mine … I feel so … relaxed. I cannot describe how it feels. He has put his other hand on my head … he is now tapping me on the chin … he is disappearing … I see a full moon." Ghouse opened his eyes then and said, simply, "I am finished. It is over."

I was surprised. This was the first time a client had been so clear and decisive that what he was receiving was complete. Both Ghouse and I were moved by his experience. As we talked, he said he was unable to find any words to describe the feeling he had when the old man held him. "It was just indescribable."

Ghouse was very sure that he was being healed. I had more questions for him than he had for me. I asked him what the letters were that he saw below the cross. Again he said that although he was familiar with a number of foreign languages, he had no idea what these symbols were. He drew them for me saying, "I think one digit is missing."

I asked him if he had asked the old man for help to go down to him and he replied, "I didn't have to. The old man looked up at me and met my eyes. He gestured with his eyes for me to come down. As he lowered his eyes, I floated down to him."

"Did the old man have a message for you, Ghouse?"

"The old man said, 'The purpose of your life is ... *The purpose of your life is solved.* Completed.'"

With that enigmatic comment, Ghouse bade me goodbye without further discussion. He did, however, make another appointment, which I looked forward to.

Second Session, Two Days Later

When Ghouse returned for his second appointment, he informed me, "I accept that Ma is no more. I also have been praying when I go to bed, as you suggested, and I'm getting a good night's sleep." I have no recollection of mentioning this to Ghouse, nor is it something I would say to a client. At that time, I was not great at praying myself, so I would not be so hypocritical as to advocate praying to anyone else. Ghouse, however, was adamant that he had heard it. He also told me that on the previous day, he and his wife had found a new house; it was not the perfect house they had imagined, but it was a start, at last.

As I studied his face, I noted that Ghouse's eyes were much clearer; much of the pain I had observed previously had gone. He also reported, "I used to get a pain here (indicating the region of his gall bladder) once or twice a day. In the last two days, I have only had the pain twice. I am feeling a little cooler."

This second session was again powerful, though comparatively speaking, not as dramatic as the first. Ghouse continued to see images throughout, seeing the crucifix three times and entering a church twice. During this session, Ghouse witnessed a beautiful scene. He described a blue sea so calm and clear that he could see the sand on the ocean floor. Later, I gave Ghouse my typed record of this second session for confirmation and approval, and he advised me that I had omitted some of the experience. He subsequently provided the following addendum:

"The water is without waves, and multicolored fish swim around the calm blue water. It is just like I am flying. I'm flying to a place where there is a hill. I am on top of the hill, and I can hear a church bell ringing. I am flying into the church. I see Christ on the cross, and then outside the church I see a woman standing at the edge of the hill; her hair is flying in the gentle breeze, and I see so much sadness on her face. Now I am back in the church. There is prayer going on. The prayer is now complete and everyone is coming out. I also fly out. I see the woman dead, lying on the shore. I fly back to the church and am crying and praying for the woman. I see a very, very bright light. The light is traveling out of the church. I follow it, and when I get out of the church, I see the woman walking into a beautiful garden that is beside the shore."

It was during this second session that Ghouse realized that he was hurting someone with his behavior. He admitted during our review, "I think I'm hurting my wife." I asked him to pay more attention to the underlying feelings behind his behavior to his partner. I gave him a very simple yoga exercise, the tree pose, to help center him physically and emotionally. I told him to stand on one leg, raising the other toward the standing thigh, and then to raise both hands, palms facing each other above the head. This posture is a wonderful aid in balancing the body, and it helps quiet the mind. It also is a useful practice for older people to help maintain balance. In addition, I introduced him to a powerful NLP (neuro linguistic programming) exercise, as outlined below, to use whenever he felt negative stress affecting him.

I asked Ghouse to revisit the scene he had been part of in the previous session, to see the calming beauty of it, to recall how the scene made him feel in his body, and to consciously feel the peace it had brought him. At precisely the same time that he was re-experiencing this sense of peace, I asked him to select an "anchor" that would help him capture the experience. The anchor he chose was to touch his forefinger gently to the thumb on both hands. He did this to demonstrate. I asked him to complete the exercise twice more with different calming and healing experiences, suggesting that the old man he met be one of them. I advised that it is important each time to use the same anchor. Then, any time he felt negative stress, he could simply connect his forefingers to his thumbs to trigger the anchor and to achieve the familiar feeling of equilibrium.

This lovely and simple exercise can be done with anyone. A word of warning: I once did it prior to going for a job interview. I did not get the job, and when I received feedback, it surprised me. My interviewer said I was acting as if I were "far too laid back." I had overdone the exercise! Before Ghouse left, I asked him to record what was happening in his life immediately preceding getting a pain signal in his liver/gall bladder area. I suspected that it only occurred when his immediate environment emotionally disturbed him. He agreed to pay more attention to this occurrence.

Third Session, Three Days Later

Ghouse was thirty minutes late for our session. Because my schedule was tight that day, I did not carry out my usually thorough review of any changes he had experienced. He complained of the same pain in his liver/gall bladder area, and I asked when it had started and, more importantly, what had preceded it. He could not identify any particular negative emotion or stress. On the positive side, this was the first time he had had the pain in three days. I am convinced that the occurrence of pain was related to Ghouse's emotional state. He did report, however, that since the last treatment, he had felt more calm and composed.

What do you want from this treatment? What do you want to be different when you leave this room?"

As he pointed toward the liver/gall bladder region, he replied, "I want to be rid of the pain."

"Is there anything else you want from this session, Ghouse?"

Ghouse referred to a confidential personal issue and said he did not wish it to happen again.

"And what do you want to receive in order that it does not happen again?"

When again he referred to what he did not want, I told him, "That is what you do not want, Ghouse."

I made a shape of a bowl with my hands and held them open toward him and said, "What is it that you want to receive?" as I gestured with my open palms.

"I want to receive love."

"Perfect. Let's start."

Ghouse made himself comfortable on the couch. Once again, I gently commenced my work, asking one of my usual questions, "Where do you feel it in your body, Ghouse?"

He did not reply to the question. Instead, I was surprised to hear him say, "It's three hundred years ago, the soldiers are everywhere … horses are traveling out from a fort … I am in a marketplace … I see an old lady … she is sitting down, and people are all around her … they are asking her something … she has answered them, and now they are all going away … the old lady is going into a hut … I am in the hut. It has one small window … I see some green bushes … I see an old man sitting."

Silence followed. At the mention of an old man, I immediately recalled his first session. I asked, "What does he look like, Ghouse?" Waiting to hear if it was the same "old man," I was excited at the prospect that he might meet him again. He continued.

> "So nice to see his face … He has a small beard. He has long hair. Kate! It's the same man I saw before … there is wisdom on his face … He is sitting on a rock … my head is on his knees … I am crying. He has his hand on my head … I am crying … He's saying, 'Son, don't worry, I am with you.' He is slowly lifting my face to him. 'Son, don't worry, I am with you … I test people, but only those whom I love … be confident … I'll always be with you.' He is standing in front of me … He blessed me, Kate … His hand is still on my head. 'Get back … I'll always be with you … Don't worry about anything … Get back.'"

After some moments, Ghouse said, "He has disappeared. I'm back." Then he made a surprising comment as he indicated the window adjacent to him, one that was shut tight against mosquito entry. "I just came back in through that window."

With a sigh, Ghouse opened his eyes and slowly raised himself to a sitting position on the couch. Once again, he had instinctively known that his experience was complete. Ghouse appeared slightly dazed, his eyes moist with tears. I watched as one single tear escaped unheeded down his right cheek. I was grateful to have been part of this new and extraordinary experience, of being witness to the love that had enabled Ghouse to free his emotions and receive love. Following the session, he looked radiant. As we discussed what had occurred, Ghouse asked, "What did he mean when he said he was testing me?"

"I'm not sure, Ghouse, but sometimes the things that happen in our lives can surely test us."

A few days later, while reading Rick Warren's book, *The Purpose Driven Life*, I was reminded that the Bible contains over two hundred references to God's testing us. I referred Ghouse to this book. As we completed our work together, I suggested that Ghouse consider working therapeutically with his partner.

Fourth Session, Three Weeks Later

With Ghouse's life seemingly changing so rapidly, I had not planned to see him again. He received a promotion in his work, he was in the process of moving to the new house, and his difficulties now seemed to have diminished or dissipated. On my return to Bangalore some weeks later, however, I agreed to schedule another session. When we talked on the phone, he reported that he was sleeping well and feeling calm and peaceful. The physical pain he had complained of in the gall bladder area had also gone. For my part, I had no real therapeutic reason to treat him, just a desire to reinforce the positive changes that had occurred since we first met. I was also selfishly excited about the prospect of being part of another deep and moving experience for Ghouse.

Ghouse looked happy and relaxed when he arrived, so different from the mental image I remembered of our first encounter weeks ago. His eyes were bright and alive. His smile was all-encompassing and full of warmth. With a great deal of pleasure, I recorded the many positive changes in his life and asked him what he wished for in the session.

"Peace and self-love. To forgive others and myself."

Beginning to work, I asked the by-now familiar question, "Do you feel any sensations, Ghouse?" Instead of answering, he started describing what he saw.

"Long, too long ... out of room ... I see tall trees ... I am in a jungle ... sheep ... flying on top of jungle ... waterfalls ... I'm slowing down into a small village ... all the people are going into a hut as before ... all the people are sitting in rows. Now I see an old man ... He's wearing pure white clothes ... long dark hair with beard ... so much peace in his eyes ... so, so much peace. He has a stick in his hand. Here is a man in the crowd ... He is struggling with so much stomach pain ... The old man is calling him to come, but he is restless with pain—he cannot walk. The old man is very gentle and taking him close to him. The old man is putting his hand on his stomach ... what a miracle ... The pain is gone … He is feeling perfectly okay. Now strong peace coming in. Everyone's closing their eyes. A ball of light is taking the old man somewhere … the light is taking him to a cave … I am there. The cave is very large … it's very black, dark. The light fills the whole cave. It is a very powerful light … now the light is writing something on the rock face in the cave … it's like a laser beam."

"What does the writing say, Ghouse?" I waited with anticipation.

"It's in a different language."

"From the place you are in the moment, do you know the meaning of the words, Ghouse?" I was referring to his level of consciousness at that precise time.

"So much is written on the rock … ten lines. The light has disappeared. The old man is slowly going toward the rock, gently touching the letters that the light has written. He's using both hands, and now he is reading it. I'm trying to read it, but the old man is stopping me … he has read everything. Now he is bending and picking up the stick that he had … walking out of the cave and going back to the small village. The entire village is coming toward him. He is looking at them and smiling. He tells them 'Get back to work.' He's going back into the hut. He knows I am watching … I'm flying inside the hut … He is looking at me … He has just brought me down. Now I am sitting in front of him. He's looking at me … lovely, beautiful eyes, so much peace … calm … looking at me and slowly putting something inside me … something coming out of his eyes and getting inside me. Now he is standing. I'm kneeling down … He's putting his right hand on my head. He tells me, 'Go back.' Again he tells me, 'Go back.' Now my leg is going back from the sea … My leg is slowly coming back … It's come back."

With that last sentence, Ghouse simultaneously opened his eyes.

When I asked Ghouse to describe the old man, he told me that he was heavily built, between fifty-five and fifty-eight years old, and had long black hair. I have no doubt that this occurrence happened exactly as Ghouse related it.

A year later, Ghouse journeyed through time yet again during a session. These mystical experiences challenged my previous belief system about the linear measurement of time. The past is no longer something I can visualize "behind" me, but rather, in some incomprehensible and inextricable way, it is part of the present.

As my work progressed, I later could also accept the visions of past loved ones appearing during healing sessions. Thanks to my work with

Rose and her son and others with similar experiences, I have been able to fit that into my expanding knowledge base and belief system. Having been so spiritually close to my father following his death, these particular experiences did not challenge me. But as I write down Ghouse's experiences for you, I have no easy explanation. In fact, I have given up any attempts to have one.

Conclusion: The End is But the Beginning

My desire in writing this book has been to support a new experience of the source of all. I call this source God, but whatever you call the higher power, I have wanted to suggest to you that it is one of non-judgment and unconditional love that is constantly at our side.

I have experienced so much in my work during the last ten years, and most, if not all, of my experiences I cannot explain categorically. I honor my clients' experiences. The comment, "It's their imagination," has been used many times to explain the phenomena my clients have experienced. When we use our imaginations, we are doing something. I encourage my clients to stop *doing* and to cease their cogitative processes beyond basic recognition and reporting. As soon as they attempt to "figure out" what is occurring, their visions cease. My clients see and hear during our work together with senses that the majority of us do not connect with or perhaps lost connection with in early childhood. They "see" previously unrecognized colors, animals, and beings—beings that are here among us. Can this be so simply explained with, "It's their imagination?"

Why am I so convinced when I claim to be a skeptic? Simply because I have witnessed men and women from across the world replicate hard-to-believe experiences. My early schooling with my "Purple People," a grounded, intelligent group, led me to accept increasingly inexplicable experiences that defied logic, such as traveling outside the body during sessions, feeling individual body parts impossibly turn as if on a spit, watching limbs disappear, and seeing differing images through each eye simultaneously. One woman actually saw a picture of her present difficult situation through her right eye while she could simultaneously see a picture of her potential future, should she choose it, through the left. This is a phenomenon that scientists would say is impossible, yet time and time again clients would describe "seeing" something, usually colors, through a single eye.

It is now commonplace in my work for my clients to meet with God in his various guises. In India, almost all of my clients see a being they identify as spirit, often the old man, Jesus, or God. The all-encompassing message in all these meetings is one of unconditional love and compassion. For those of us who were brought up to believe in judgment and retribution, meeting a humorous God of pure love, compassion, and joy is a wonder indeed. Perhaps it also creates a challenge. What order would the world be in if it weren't for our fear of judgment? Without judgment, would we run amok? If only we could turn that long held view around and see how joyful life could be if we insisted on focusing on love and forgiveness. Was forgiveness not the last message Jesus left us with from the cross? He said, "Father, forgive them, for they know not what they do."

I have excluded a few of the occurrences I have been party to over recent years from this book, not because I doubted my clients, but because I felt their experiences were just too much for my readers to accept. Maybe I do you, the reader, an injustice. If so, I apologize. It was a calculated decision. I feel so strongly that *Healing Visions* has an important message to impart, and I edited accordingly.

I have already started work on my next book, *Who Am I?* Some of the omitted pieces from this book will find a home in the next one. Included will be the story of Devi, who has met beings not of this world who are here to guide us; the story of Ayesha, who has been invited into spaceships on two occasions; and my work with embodied angels who relate how difficult it is for them to be here on earth. I will also include my clients' experiences of performing their own psychic surgery.

As I open more and more to the connection I have and continue to evolve, I know my clients will receive and experience that much more, as well.

We are on the cusp of great changes in our lives here on planet Earth. Time, place, our senses, and communication as we know it are all being challenged and are no longer static or measurable. There is much excitement ahead.

Love,

Kate

PS: I remain the Skeptical Healer.

Printed by W&G Baird Ltd.

ISBN: 978-0-9567999-1-3